Goldensun

Also by Rich Castro

Extracted

Defiance

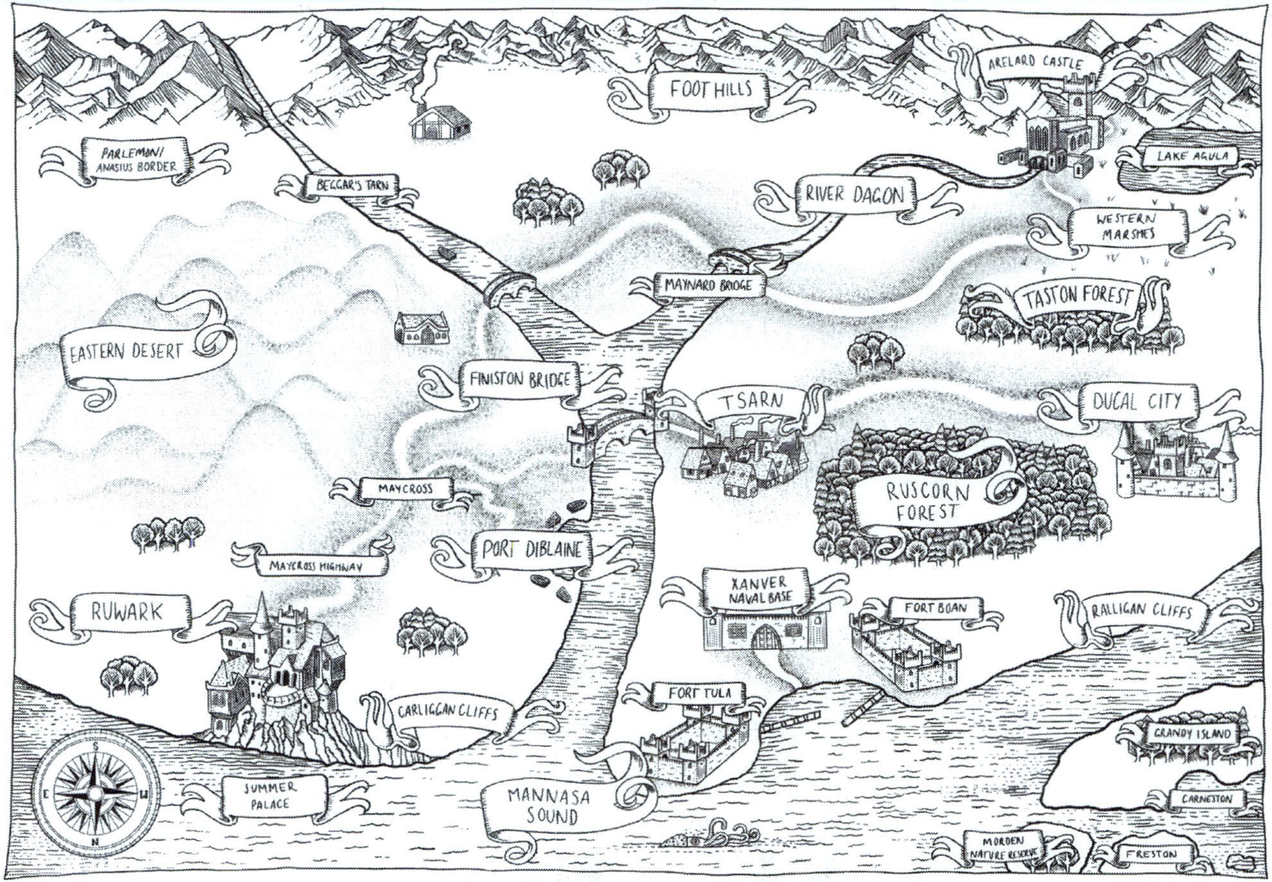

Foot Hills
Arelard Castle
Parlemon/ Anasius Border
Beggar's Tarn
Lake Agula
River Dagon
Western Marshes
Maynard Bridge
Taston Forest
Eastern Desert
Finiston Bridge
Tsarn
Ducal City
Ruscorn Forest
Maycross
Port Diblaine
Maycross Highway
Xanver Naval Base
Fort Boan
Ruwark
Ralligan Cliffs
Fort Tula
Carliggan Cliffs
Grandy Island
Summer Palace
Mannasa Sound
Carneston
Morden Nature Reserve
Freston
S
W
E
N

1

The Order of the Dragon

Hera's short blonde hair spiked upwards towards the leaden sky, accentuating the steely determination in her eyes as the horn sounded for the fight to begin. She sparred with her opponent, feeling him out and hunting for weaknesses. Their feet moved constantly as they lunged and ducked and feinted and whirled. Young as she was at thirteen, Hera's relentless training had already provided her slim figure with well-toned muscle and rapid reaction time.

Suddenly, Janus thrust his lance forwards towards her torso, but he was far too slow to catch her off guard. Her lightning sidestep and counterthrust resulted in a guttural grunt from Janus as he took the full weight of her cudgel in his midriff. He bent over and retreated a step to regain his breath and his balance. But Hera did not allow him the privilege. She lunged forwards and delivered a second blow to his chest, sending him sprawling, gasping for air. He rolled over, clutching his chest and grasping for his lance. But Hera kicked it away from his hand, disarming him. She stood over him, waiting for him to rise. The horn sounded again, and the bout was over. Janus lay panting, his perspiration mingling with the dust. Hera had not even broken a sweat.

The tournament was in its early stages, and most of the newcomers were knocked out in the first two rounds. Janus, though, had been with the Order of the Dragon for three years and he thought he had made progress. This devastating defeat at the hands of Hera made him realise how far he had yet to go. He had known she was going to win the round before the bell had even tolled to signal its start, but he thought he may at least have given her a run for her money. As he picked himself up and gazed around the sparsely populated arena, he reckoned that Hera's only chance of defeat would come from one of the Seniors. She might even make it into the semi-finals which would be a record-breaking achievement for a Shell. But then...she'd been here a long time.

Later that evening, Hera lay in her bunk, reminiscing about years gone by. Inevitably, her thoughts led her to the night of her kidnap eight years earlier. The details were seared into her brain. The family to whom she once belonged were sleeping in the house as she was woken and whisked from her bed, blankets and all, tape fixed firmly across her mouth to prevent her from making a noise. She remembered that terrifying journey in the blackness of the van, and the smell of fumes and oil and sawdust and urine. She remembered the blinding light that greeted her as the doors opened in the delivery dock at the far end of the compound. She remembered her terror as warriors clad in black pulled her from the van and put her on the docking platform to be inspected. She remembered how she had stood in her damp pink nightgown, biting her lip and refusing to cry, glaring back at them in hostility. She remembered that throughout her first year here she had refused to speak, refused to trust anyone, withdrew deep within herself. But she never forgot her parents and her little brother Jethry.

Most trainees arrived at the compound around the age of nine, orphaned by accident or design. Usually they came loudly, with heart-rending sobs, screaming at the monks. Often it took months for them to calm down and become useful. But Hera had been only five years old when she was taken. Within days, she had adjusted to a new life in the compound – perhaps it was because she was so young. Within two weeks, she was knuckling down to train. She never cried. She never looked back. She built a wall around her heart and pushed the pain away. No-one would ever break her. She would never surrender. And she would be the best warrior the Order of the Dragon had ever seen.

She remembered the night, three years later, when she had finally figured out how to exit her dormitory via the skylight and get across the compound unnoticed in the dark. Now she could watch the Seniors do their advanced combat training. After that, night after night, she would lie in the shadows on the rooftop, memorising the moves and methods the monks were teaching. Then, early in the morning – as she moved out of the dormitory for the strictly regulated ten-minute shower in the wash hut – she would rehearse those same moves in the large cubicle, the running water to her left covering the sounds of her feet on the boards. Then she would jump under the water and race through the shower in the last ninety seconds, pulling her clothes over her not-quite-dry body, and emerge panting into the compound ready for the day's work. She smiled as she remembered that she had kept this up for nearly eighteen months before someone discovered she was not in her bed when she should have been. Then there was hell to pay.

She turned over on her bed once more, searching for a cool place on her pillow on the hot April evening, trying to get to sleep. She could hear a few of the Shells discussing the tournament and the Narkon Carnival that accompanied it. It was the one time of the year all the trainees enjoyed. The flamboyant market stalls with their wide range of hats and artwork and clothing and ornaments and fruit and candy. The performers on stilts who wove in and out of the crowds, juggling fire sticks or riding unicycles. The giant animal balloons in impossible colours, desperately held down by beefy men in striped shirts and rippling brown capes. The massive model dragon flowing up and down the street, powered by twenty Senior combatants dressed in deep vermillion robes. The musicians dotted about the town, playing their jaunty tunes on traditional Turonian instruments. The smells from the pop-up grills churning out huge quantities of pan-seared wings and pork ribs, all devoured by the happy and hungry crowds surging across the town. The trainees loved the carnival. With so many bustling crowds and so much noise, it was the easiest thing in the world to steal food from the grills and the tubs of candy and the fruit and vegetable stalls and the international cuisine marquees and most of the other food vendors who were crammed into every nook and cranny of the cobbled streets. It was the one and only time of the year that the trainees could have full bellies.

Hera heard the other Shells making their carnival plans. But she knew that if she wanted to win, she could take no part in the carnival. The tournament was all that mattered. Unusually, she and one other Shell had progressed to the second day of fighting. Tomorrow the arena would be full by midday with all the senior city leaders in the VIP box watching to see who would be crowned the winner. The dividing barriers in the arena would be removed for the final three rounds of competition so that the spectators could give each fight their undivided attention. The royal band would be playing on the podium at one end. The royal visitors would process to the Royal Box followed by their retinue of dignitaries and bodyguards and personal attendants. And the bell would toll.

Hera tried to push it from her mind, and she turned over once more, willing herself to sleep. But she could not help dreaming of glory. What if she made it to the quarter-finals? What if she broke the record and made the semi-finals? What if she won? Surely, she would get an assignment then? But over the past twenty years, only Seniors had ever won. They were taller, broader, stronger and had more years of training behind them. It was inevitable. And yet...She tossed about on the bed, finding it difficult to get comfortable, to relax, to rest. The Shells around her had stopped their murmuring and the dormitory was quiet. But it had been dark for some time before Hera finally slept. It was a good thing she did not know what tomorrow would bring.

2

The Second Day

Hera awoke to leaden gloom, with the rain falling on the skylight. This was not the gentle pattering of a light shower, nor the heavy hammering of a passing downpour. Rather, it was a relentless drumming on glass, a steady and committed driving rain that was in for the long haul. She grinned to herself in the half-darkness. Rain meant she had an advantage. In the rain, Seniors were nervous of slipping, especially with high kicks and swinging lunges. And as a lighter and more agile combatant, her chances were marginally higher. The difference was almost imperceptible. But it was there. She climbed down from her bunk and prepared herself for the day ahead.

Two hours later, she was in one of the dressing rooms in the bowels of the arena. There were no windows, only strong lights, black walls and gaudy paintings of former Turonian warriors standing over their defeated foes. There were long counters with make-up trays and sinks and hair products and huge mirrors surrounded in gold mouldings. There were racks carrying breeches and capes and tight leggings and base layers and stockings and scarves and stretch tops. There were stands holding lances and spears and cudgels and battle axes. There were rows of body armour and ancient mail shirts and leather forearm protectors. Unlike in times past, most warriors arrived with everything they needed, their combat attire carefully checked, documented and approved before they ever reached the dressing rooms. But occasionally, usually for superstitious reasons, a combatant would select an item from the dressing rooms – perhaps a couple of gartered stockings or a ribbon.

Hera had a simple approach to attire. She rejected everything flamboyant – no capes or flowing robes, no spears or axes, no restrictive body armour. Instead, Hera went bare-headed and wore only a body-hugging top, leggings, a forearm protector and a brace to counter the weight of the medium-length cudgel which swung from her wrist. She dressed the same way for every fight – simple, unadorned, ready. The only thing she took time over was the spikes of her hair. She waxed them until they were stuck straight out from her head like the quills of a porcupine as it took up a defensive pose. No-one else prepared for battle like she did.

Out in the arena, a huge Order of the Dragon banner hung outside the stadium and the majestic golden dragon standard fluttered from the flagpole high above the Royal Box, visible from most of the town. But the walk into the arena on the second day was very different from the first. On day one, only the monks and perhaps a couple of hundred local spectators were scattered in groups around the stadium. Yesterday, gentle music was being piped through the speakers as the combatants fought for glory, but there was no applause, no cheering from the crowd, no sense of atmosphere.

The second day, however, was a completely contrasting story. Despite the driving rain, two-thirds of the stadium was filled with spectators by mid-morning, and more were coming. The retractable roof had been pulled across the stands, and the floodlights provided much-needed illumination of the contestants. Long-range cameras caught the detail of the action and relayed it onto the huge screens at each end of the arena. The crowd sang and roared and laughed and booed and rippled like waves on a rough sea. The VIP box was filled, and the Royal Box was being prepared for the arrival not only of the Emperor, but also of his royal guests from Notalia, Anasius and Parlemoni. The Royal Tattoo, a huge band of over 200 instrumentalists, were already entertaining the crowds with live music, from old Turonian classics to the more modern "fizz" music enjoyed by so many of the country's young people.

Hera walked through the tunnel and into the stadium along with the thirty-one remaining combatants. She was watching them carefully, trying to anticipate the ones she would have to fight and what their weak points might be. Juntox, the only other Shell through to the fifth round, was garrulous.

"I wonder who we'll be fighting first," he said. "Do you think they'll go easy on us and give us those two skinny ones over there?" He pointed ahead to two Junior twin boys. "I mean, it would be wrong to make us fight Seniors for the first battle of the day, don't you think? Just look at that guy." He nodded off to his right at a bearded Senior who must have been six feet tall and almost half as wide. "He's terrifying. I wonder what he's been eating—"

"—Shhhh," Hera quelled him. Juntox always talked when he was nervous. She was trying to stay focused.

As they emerged into the bright lights of the stadium and the pouring rain, the band reached a crescendo and the crowd erupted in applause, whistles and cheering. This was their first glimpse of the top contestants from the Order of the Dragon this year. They knew the list of names, and many had read the brief synopsis of each player and placed their bets accordingly. The way the betting worked meant that all those who backed the right player received a cut of the full pot of prize money. There was no payout for second place, and there was a great deal of money involved. A successful bet here would ensure financial security for a winning punter, probably for the rest of their lives. As a result, there was much interest in the combatants as they arrived. Some warriors had fought in previous contests, but for others, this was the first time they had been seen in the public arena.

The combatants came to a halt at the red line as the crowd continued to express itself through the stamping of feet and clapping of hands and the screaming of youngsters and the whistles and cheering of others. The combatants stood stock-still, keeping their faces expressionless as they had been taught. They worked to keep the fear and nerves out of their eyes as the cameras moved systematically down the line, pausing for a few seconds on each face as the commentators reiterated their names and some of their background, before moving to the next one. Finally, the noise of the crowd began to subside, and the combatants were given the signal to form four perfectly spaced straight lines opposite the Royal Box. The Royal Tattoo then struck up the royal anthem to greet the Emperor, whilst his guests and the crowd rose to their feet out of respect.

The cannons around the roof of the stadium fired their blank rounds in swift succession, their sound ricocheting around the arena. In the middle of this, the Emperor and his royal entourage drove into the arena in the famed golden carriage pulled by four magnificent black stallions. Their coats were brushed and gleaming and their bridles and bits glistened under the glare of the floodlights. The carriage came to a stop directly below the Royal Box and an immaculately dressed attendant skipped across to open the door with a flourish and a bow.

The Emperor stepped out onto the first step, gave a royal wave to the tumultuous crowd and then descended to the floor. The anthem came to an end, the combatants bowed in homage and guests got settled in their plush seats.

"Welcome to the second day of the tournament of the year 561," the Emperor spoke into the microphone before him, his voice cutting through the downpour. "On behalf of the Order of the Dragon, let opponent selection begin." Then he pressed the large red button in front of him and the giant screens exploded into life once more, showing the names of all thirty-two candidates as they were shuffled randomly into place. At that moment, Juntox and Hera realised that whether or not they progressed to the final sixteen depended entirely upon blind, pitiless chance. They held their breath.

Within moments, the shuffling slowed and the names settled into the slots. Juntox would fight Magna, a tall olive-skinned Junior girl with long black hair wound up into a tight bun on the top of her head. Magna took a sidewise glace at Juntox just down the line from him and grinned. In that second, any hope Juntox had previously held died a swift death.

Hera was to fight Marcus who was a short stocky Senior, built like a tank. Juntox gave her a thinly veiled smile of encouragement, but Hera could see the doubt in his eyes.

Following allocation came the fight order selection. For this the fourth round, two fights would happen simultaneously, one at each end of the stadium. Juntox's fight was fifth and Hera's was seventh. They were secretly glad they were not called to fight each other, or to fight at the same time – it meant they could watch each other's work.

"Let battle commence!" The Emperor's voice came over the speakers once more.

3

Valour, Victory and Pain

A lone bugler from the Royal Tattoo sounded the four familiar notes to signal the start of the contest. With two fights to watch at the same time, and fights lasting a maximum of ten minutes each, time flew.

Juntox talked constantly, describing what was happening, wondering about who was likely to progress to the last sixteen and who was "definitely going out." It was a vaguely comforting monotone in the background as Hera focused on her opponent and tried to recall what she had seen of his fighting back in the compound as she had watched him from the rooftop.

The previous evening, she had listed each contestant and tried to remember their strengths and weaknesses. She had watched footage of each one fighting earlier in the year and had studied their track records and their achievements and failures. She had tried to commit all that information to her memory. But now, with the noise of the crowd and the tattoo and the bright lights, her nerves were making it hard to breathe, let alone remember anything. She drew in a long, deep breath.

"Magna and Juntox," came the call over the speakers. Juntox stopped talking.

"Wish me well." His face was pale.

"May good fortune be yours," she said, giving a weak smile. She didn't know how wishing him good fortune was going to make the slightest difference to his pending defeat, but it was the thing to say. Then Juntox and Magna were striding towards the ring furthest from the Royal Box, led by two vermillion-clad monks who were instructing them as they went.

Hera watched as they moved to the plate and waited for the horn. Despite the lashing rain, Magna looked business-like and perfectly poised. Juntox's shaking knees were visible even from this distance. The horn sounded.

Magna stepped forward, waved her baton, and then spun on her left heel before driving her right foot outwards towards Juntox's chest. He tried to jump backwards out of the way, but he was not quite fast enough. The heel of Magna's foot punched into his stomach, driving the air from his lungs, making him double over and gasp with the pain.

"Get round, get round!" Hera heard herself shouting, anticipating Magna's next move accurately. Miraculously, Juntox gathered himself together and whirled to his right, Magna's baton missing his head by inches. He swung out with his left hand as her arm moved past his head, delivering a driving blow to her right shoulder. She cried out in surprise but was facing him again in a moment. The fighting was relentless now, but her superior height and speed meant that for all his efforts, Juntox was only delaying the inevitable. Hera knew it. Magna knew it. Juntox knew it. It took her less than three minutes to send Juntox sprawling into the dirt, and she had delivered a second and third blow before he could even begin to get back to his feet. The horn sounded again. Magna had won. The crowd roared.

Juntox clawed his way off the wet ground, blood trickling from his nose. He bowed groggily before being led back to the group, the red loser's tag fastened around his right wrist. As he passed, he met Hera's eye. "Issshup to you now," he slurred.

After the intervening fight, Hera heard her name called and she was led across to the nearest ring alongside Marcus. The rain was just beginning to ease off now, but it was still leaving a slick layer across her face. But visibility was okay. She watched how he moved, and whilst he worked hard to hide it, she noticed a very slight lift in his lower right leg. He had sustained an injury from the day before. She allowed herself a shiver of satisfaction. There was hope.

Standing at the plate beneath the lights was a surreal moment. The crowd were restless, waiting for the fights to begin. Moments passed. Then, like an extended thunderclap in the night, the horn sounded its four notes, loud and demanding. Marcus was stepping forward to make the first move. His weapon of choice was a thick leather strap which Hera eyed nervously.

Hera ducked and whirled, demonstrating that she was by far the nimblest of the two, but she knew she would never win if she didn't go on the offensive. She feigned a kick to her left but thrust her baton out and upwards into his chest as he dodged to the right. It was the first blow to land, and although it did little damage, it made him angry. The leather strap flew in all directions and Marcus managed to catch Hera across the back of her left arm as she strove to evade him. She cried out in pain but refused to back off. She dived to the muddy ground as he moved to his left, making him stumble over her prone figure. She leapt to her feet and delivered another blow, this time from her right foot into his left side as he scrambled to rise again.

Minutes later both were panting hard, covered in dirt, exploring each other's strengths and hunting for weaknesses. A sudden lash of the strap and the leather rammed down hard onto the baton in Hera's hand. Already slippery, she dropped it. And now she was weaponless against this wall of muscle and his ferocious whip. She tried a high kick towards his chin, but he dodged it, grinning at her and raising his arm for another lash with his leather strap. In that moment, she saw her chance. She raised her right arm to receive the lash but, at the same time, stomped with all her weight onto his right instep. For Marcus, the dull aching injury from the day before suddenly exploded into a deep pain he could not ignore. His face changed as he crumpled onto his right knee. The lash drew blood from Hera's arm, but she ignored it. She spun to her left and delivered a second blow with her left foot to Marcus' jaw. He crashed to the ground, unsure what had happened to him, dizzy and trying to clear his head. A final blow to his midriff seconds later sealed his defeat. The horn sounded. Somehow, Hera had survived the onslaught. The crowd bellowed its excitement. Punters checked their lists. Cheering echoed around the stadium. A Shell had made it to the last sixteen. People were taking notice. Perhaps this would be a history-making year? Interest in Hera surged. In the Royal Box, Prince Grayson pointed her out to the Emperor. "One to watch," he said.

After that, the fights came quickly. Next, in the last sixteen, Hera was drawn with a spindly Junior girl who had somehow made it through the previous round more by luck than skill. Hera dealt with her within two minutes. In the quarter-finals she had her work cut out for her and used every ounce of her energy to get the better of a Senior by the name of "Scotty". He was a bully, though, and she knew that bullies are often more mouth than might. So it proved and then, for the first time in living memory, there was a Shell in the last four. She was the talk of the crowd, who sang and roared and cheered and clapped and sang again.

Pausing for a moment, Hera tried to recover herself. There were ugly welts on both her arms from Marcus' leather strap. Her nose was bleeding, her left leg was shaking from a devastating kick she had sustained in the last round, and she was fast developing a black eye from an elbow to her face by the skinny girl. Hera looked more fit for a hospital than a fight, but she stood poker-faced as she waited for her name to be called once more.

The stewards had rearranged the arena so that there was just one ring in the centre of the stadium with all the cameras now trained upon it. For the final three battles, the combatants would have the undivided attention of the whole crowd. The Royal Tattoo were playing more of the old classics now, and the crowd were in good voice. Hera looked over to the screen and saw the faces of each of the four combatants. It took her a few moments before she realised that the girl with the bloodied face, black eye and matted hair was, in fact, her.

"It looks much worse than it is," she reminded herself. In fact, maybe it was an advantage. "The others will think I am weak when, in fact, I'm as strong as I've ever been." It was not entirely true, but it seemed to help her to stand taller and ignore the pain.

It turned out that her fight was the second of the two semi-finals, so she had to wait for over fifteen minutes before she was called. In the interim, she watched the first battle between two Seniors, both male and both well over six feet tall. The one with the weedy moustache and the dark green eyes held a long blunt spear in his left hand and wore a black headband to keep his bushy hair out of his eyes. He had beaten Magna to reach this point. The other fighter, Zoran, was a ferocious warrior, clad in black leather, bare-headed and armed with a short stubby bar. As the horn sounded for their fight to begin, Hera was glad she had some time to recover and to call to mind her own opponent's strengths and weaknesses.

He was a tall, mild-mannered and well-built Senior whose dark-skinned muscles rippled and shone with sweat from the round before. He looked totally calm and composed and, to Hera's surprise, he was smiling, as if amused by the antics of the warriors in the ring. Hera knew she needed a strategy, but her fuzzy head was struggling to think. Besides, whenever she looked at him, her heart twisted in ways she wasn't used to, and she found herself wishing he would turn to look at her too. That wasn't good. She decided to avoid looking at him and to concentrate instead on what she knew of his tactics from back in the compound. She remembered how fast he was, and how devastating his work was with the weighted alpenstock he favoured. She fought down her fear and tried to calm her pounding heart. He seemed impenetrable.

The horn sounded and moustache guy was in the dirt, struggling to rise. Zoran stood triumphant in his black leather. And now it was time. Two monks led Hera and her opponent across to the ring, passing the previous two fighters on the way. She stepped to the plate. The sound of the crowd died away. Even the rain had stopped. She felt the whole world hold its breath. Would she be the first Shell ever to make it to the final of the tournament? She drove the enormity of it from her mind and forced herself to focus. And then, for her, the whole world contracted. There was one ring. One opponent. One goal. Nothing more. No noise. No crowd. No arena. No tournament. Just her opponent standing between her and the final. She had one job to do. The horn cut through her consciousness and the fight began.

The Senior was staring at her, his dark brown eyes boring into her soul. She couldn't hold his gaze. They sparred left and right and left again, feeling each other out, hunting for weaknesses. She knew he was sizing her up, examining her injuries to see which might give him an advantage. Her arms hurt from the welts, but they had not lost their strength. She knew, though, that her left leg was vulnerable. Something in her movement must have given her away, because suddenly he knew it as well. And try as she might, she could not find one chink in his armour. Despite the intensity of the battle, his face was open with that slight faraway smile. He seemed both supremely confident of his win and yet, at the same time, almost...apologetic? She shook her head clear. Stop analysing him. Focus. What to do?

She delivered the first blow to the back of his hand as she ducked beneath his alpenstock. His eyebrows went up, but he didn't hesitate in whirling around and throwing a kick towards her midriff. She threw her body to the side, but the force of his foot glancing off her left side was enough to wind her. She sucked in air and spun around once more to meet him. She was trying to use her shorter stature to her advantage by swinging her cudgel at his legs, whilst trying to protect her left leg at the same time, so it came as a complete surprise when he delivered a devastating kick to her right leg. Why would he go for her strongest side? It had never occurred to her that he would. And when he did, it felled her like a tree. She rolled to the side and bounced up to her feet as fast as she could, but as soon as she landed on her feet, she felt pain shoot up both her legs. For a brief moment it was etched into her face before she brought herself back under control. She glanced at her opponent. He had seen it.

She swung her cudgel, feinted to the right and swung it behind her, delivering an unexpected blow to his right shin. "Now it's your turn to show pain," she thought. But, somehow, impossibly, he hardly even winced. Instead, the edge of his alpenstock struck her under her right arm and sent her cudgel spinning out of the ring. The crowd roared.

She jumped around and made a few punching jabs. He dodged her easily, returning the jabs and then sending a high left kick to her left side. Hera fell again. She was losing and they both knew it. There was a huge cheer from the crowd. She looked up, and she saw his hand outstretched – an offer to help her arise. That was why the crowd had cheered. But she would never accept help from an opponent. She didn't want any pity. She was not done. She forced her body up from the floor, sidestepped her opponent's arm and twisted round to fight once more. He shrugged briefly, brought his hands up and stood ready to meet her. She was panting and sweating. He was calm as a millpond and looked like he could easily have just got up from a short nap. There was no hope. The crowd was singing again.

Hera tried a different tactic. Instead of delivering a kick, she simply threw her whole body at him, twisting in the air and falling directly into his chest. He staggered backwards but did not fall. Instead, he drove his elbow into her side, and she collapsed to the floor, gasping for air. There were fireworks in her head. She couldn't see. The horn sounded and the crowd erupted.

As she stumbled back to the fighters' quadrant at the side of the arena, she noticed the red tag secured around her right wrist. Juntox was there to greet her, but she could not look at him. She had lost.

4

The Summons

Watching the final of the tournament was an emotional whirlwind for Hera. Zoran, the warrior in black leather, fought with a vicious, relentless fury that was frightening to behold. But the dark-skinned, mild-mannered fighter who had beaten Hera, whose name turned out to be Kayton, seemed almost immune to pain. His alpenstock twirled and jumped about as he ducked and jabbed and twisted to avoid the short metal bar clenched in Zoran's right hand.

Hera watched on, her stomach swirling. Zoran's bar struck Kayton cleanly on the left wrist, and as the "crack" rippled across the arena, the crowd drew a collective gasp. A millisecond later, Kayton's alpenstock drove into the ground right beneath Zoran's feet and Kayton's full weight shouldered Zoran into it. He stumbled and fell, and it was only as Zoran was falling that Kayton allowed himself to wince at the agony that was travelling up his left forearm.

Zoran hit the dirt and blood erupted from his nose. He rolled to the side and tried to clear his head. He noticed a hand in front of him. Kayton was offering to help him rise.

Zoran growled and swirled his metal bar towards the hand. He did not need help. He rose to his feet, swaying like a ship in a boiling sea. Kayton had leapt to the side and swung around to face Zoran once more, waiting for him to steady himself. The crowd cheered its delight. It was not often that a gentleman made it to the final. This truly was a fight to watch: one fought hard and dirty whilst the other held a deep belief in chivalry and honour. The fight went on.

A few minutes later, Zoran seemed to have collected himself. His face was still dripping with blood and dirt, and his eyes were like those of a bull in the ring. Kayton was calmly sidestepping and avoiding Zoran's lunges and trying to avoid the pain in his broken wrist. Suddenly, as Zoran lunged once more, Kayton drove his alpenstock to meet Zoran's iron bar. The alpenstock snapped like a twig in a hurricane, much to Zoran's delight. But his delight was short-lived. Even as the alpenstock broke, Kayton had swung out with his left leg and drove his foot into Zoran's side. Zoran fell like a tree, and it was over. The horn sounded.

The crowd erupted. Stamping, clapping, cheering, shouting, whistling. It was pandemonium. Kayton's picture bounced onto the huge screens as the victor in the tournament of the year 561. Attendants raced across the arena floor to lift him onto the champion's litter and parade him around the stadium. Others reached Zoran to help him off the field, but he growled his refusal.

"Don't touch me," he was heard to say as he clawed to his feet and staggered towards Kayton's smiling figure. "He's mine."

But Kayton skipped nimbly towards the litter and turned to face Zoran who was now nearly upon him, attendants trailing nervously behind. The crowd quieted as the scene unfolded before them. Was there going to be a second fight? Such a lack of discipline would be hugely humiliating for the Order of the Dragon, and with neighbouring countries represented by royalty up in the Royal Box, it would be a national embarrassment. The dignitaries were looking at each other. Arena officials started to stand, unsure what to do. There was no protocol for this.

Suddenly, Kayton's voice rang out loud and clear. "Ladies and Gentlemen of Turonia!" he began. He repeated it as the crowd fell silent.

"Ladies and Gentlemen, I give you Zoran. Zoran the mighty. Zoran the ferocious. Zoran the indestructible. I may have won this competition, but in a war, it is Zoran you want on your side, not me. He never gives up. He never gives in. He refuses to back down. He continues against all odds. Most warriors would run rather than fight him. Thank you for attending the Tournament of the Order of the Dragon, and please raise a shout for Zoran who is, without a doubt, the strongest, mightiest and most fearsome warrior in all of Turonia."

Zoran's face, whilst covered in blood and grime, had a distinct look of confusion. The crown erupted again in cheers and whistles, and then, with stamping feet and deafening chant, it shouted, "Zoran! Zoran! Zoran!" Zoran's face changed, and he drove his arms into the air, receiving the applause like water to a parched traveller.

"Zoran," Kayton shouted above the noise of the crowd. "Let's do the victory lap together." He jumped up onto the litter and extended a hand to Zoran. Zoran ignored the hand and ignored Kayton, but he jumped up beside him, nonetheless. Kayton motioned to the litter bearers, and they lifted the platform carefully to their shoulders, with Kayton and Zoran on board. Kayton reached to steady the wobbling Zoran, but Zoran brushed his hand away.

"I don't need your help," he glowered before turning back to the crowd. But he was wrong. Kayton had to stop him falling on two or three occasions as they traversed the arena, despite Zoran's unfriendly protestations. Zoran thought the crowd's cheers were for him, and initially they had been. But when the crowds recognised the diplomacy and grace with which Kayton had deftly avoided a national incident, their cheering was mostly for him.

Up in the Royal Box, the Emperor and Prince Grayson looked at one another. The Emperor nodded. Prince Grayson summoned the Lord Protector and gave him his instructions.

At the end of the lap, all the warriors walked back into the tunnel and returned to the dressing rooms. The tournament of 561 was over.

Hera collected her small rucksack, took a long drink of water and prepared to return to the compound alongside Juntox, who was now far less talkative. Instead, he was nursing his various injuries and insisting that Hera visit the sanitorium to get her wrist fixed up.

It was only as she opened her bag back on her bunk that evening that she saw the small brown envelope. It was so nondescript that she almost let it slip to the floor, unnoticed. But as she pulled out the small card that lay within, her eyes opened wider and wider. She stopped breathing. The Black Ops. *She*, a thirteen-year-old girl, a mere Shell, was being summoned to train with Black Ops. She read the card again to make sure, flipping it over. But there it was, the unmistakeable Black Ops seal imprinted into the back.

She was pretty sure what they were asking was unprecedented. And she knew she couldn't tell a soul.

5

The Stray

Mark and Layla sat on a bench at West Ducal tram station, waiting for the next tram to come through. They discussed plans for the winter markets which began the following week. The market stalls were always full of such fascinating items reflecting amazing creativity from all over the southern continent, and a meander through the streets usually meant ending up with a great stock of presents for various family members. Layla loved it. Mark was less keen and, to be honest, would have preferred to sit in a coffee shop and let Layla shop alone. However, despite having very little idea about what was tasteful and what was not, he wanted to be supportive.

As they sat, they noticed a girl with short blonde hair emerge from the shadows to their right, carrying a rucksack and looking dishevelled.

"That's the third time we've seen her this week," Mark murmured. They watched for a moment longer.

"Yes." Layla responded. "She was here two days ago, same clothes too."

“How on earth do you remember that?” Mark asked, raising an eyebrow. “I can’t remember a thing.”

Layla agreed, rather too forcefully for Mark’s liking.

“My name’s Layla, by the way,” his wife of thirty-one years grinned at him. She stuck out her hand for him to shake. Mark grimaced.

“Maybe she comes here to shop? Or maybe she lives here in Ducal City?” he wondered.

“Maybe she doesn’t have anywhere to live at all. She looks mighty thin.” Layla paused and Mark knew she was thinking of their own girl, Angela, now grown and living in a different part of the country. “I’m going to ask her.” And with that, she stood up.

“Wait…” Mark began, but he was too slow.

“Hello,” Layla said warmly as the girl turned to face her with her large, uncertain eyes. “I’m Layla and this is Mark, my husband,” she added as Mark arrived beside her. “We saw you here a couple of days back. Do you live here in Ducal City?”

The girl looked proud and strong, despite her crumpled clothing. Her expression was fiery. She paused before answering in a lilting Turonian accent.

“I do live here, yes.”

Mark couldn’t think of anything to say at all, as was usual in most social situations, but his wife didn’t have such problems.

“Oh lovely, are you coming to the winter markets next week?” she asked.

“I may,” Hera said, not giving anything away.

Layla was undeterred.

"You should if you can," she said. "Last year there was a stall selling venison steaks straight from the grill, and quite cheaply too. They were amazing; I've never tasted anything quite so good as that. It was very cold, too. I remember being glad of being well wrapped up. They say the temperature is going to drop tomorrow." Layla was changing tack. "I hope you've got some warmer wear; Ducal City gets pretty cold in the winter."

Mark couldn't help but marvel at his friendly wife. Her openness was just one of the reasons he loved her – how she managed it was quite beyond him.

The girl smiled faintly as she said, "Well, I'm not sure what I'm up to next week. I tend to live one day at a time."

Layla smiled again. "Well, that's okay. I was wondering about having a drink. Would you like one?"

"Well, I...er..." Hera was unsure how to proceed with this development. She hadn't intended to talk to anyone this morning, let alone go for a drink with anyone.

"The next tram isn't for forty minutes, and we might as well be sitting comfortably having a drink instead of standing around the tram station getting bored." Layla took advantage of Hera's hesitation.

Hera nodded. She had no money herself, but neither had she managed to steal anything yet today, so she was very thirsty. Not to mention hungry.

"Mark'll sort us out," Layla assured her. "There's a great little eatery just up the stairs here, and they do little somethings as well as the usual nectar drinks." She paused, seeing the look of confusion on Hera's face. She laughed and then explained as they ascended the stairs.

"Oh yes, sorry. When my nephew was about two, we were walking through town with him and suddenly he turned his little face upwards to us and said, "Aunty, time for a little something, maybe?" It was the cutest thing. And now, whenever we go for a snack somewhere, we tend to refer to it as a little something."

It was Hera's turn to smile. It was sweet, she thought. The sort of sweetness she hadn't seen in a while. She warmed to this strange lady who had accosted her with unexpected kindness, and she felt her muscles relax a little. Hera would usually be hesitant to follow strangers, but her recent lifestyle choices were beginning to take their toll. She was tired.

"Now," Layla continued as they arrived at Hunter's Cafe, "we can sit outside here, it's not too cold at the moment." Hera managed to keep the relief out of her face as she realised she was going to get a drink and something to eat without needing to worry about paying for it.

Mark emerged from the cafe a few minutes later with three drinks and a bag of pastries. Whilst he was not great at conversation, he did make good decisions, and knowing Hera was probably very hungry, he had asked for six different pastries.

"Thank you dear," Layla said to Mark. "I was asking Hera – that's her name – whether she enjoyed our trams. She's not from here, you see."

“Oh,” Mark grunted, in between mouthfuls of pastry. Why didn’t women understand that eating was much more important than talking? Even Hera seemed to think so, judging by the speed with which she devoured her pastry. Not that Layla minded. Conversations with her were often rather one-sided anyway. Layla turned back to Hera.

“So where are you from, my dear? Your voice sounds a bit...Turonian?”

“Yes, I grew up there, although I can’t go back now. Not since...” She coughed a little, and her voice wobbled. She took a gulp of her nectar. “My folks were taken into custody last week,” she choked. “But I escaped here. I can’t go back, so I shall have to make do.”

“But Hera,” Layla looked shocked. “You’re only a girl. Where can you live? What will you eat? What school will you attend?”

“I’ll be okay,” Hera assured her. “I’m fifteen and I can take care of myself.” Lying came very easily to Hera.

Having finished his pastry, Mark found himself responding, “I think we should speak to the authorities to make sure you’re looked after properly. You can’t live in a tram station.”

“Yes, I can,” Hera contradicted him. “I’ve lived here for a week, and no-one’s complained.”

Layla touched Hera’s arm.

“We can’t let you live like this.”

“Sure you can.”

“The police need to be aware...”

"Don't," Hera started to get alarmed. There was no way the police could find her. She put down the pastry. "If you go to the authorities, they'll just return me to Turonia and make me live in an awful children's home."

"But, Hera, leaving you alone like this is wrong."

"Do you know what those children's homes are like?" Hera fixed her steely eyes on Mark and Layla, concocting the lie as she spoke. "If you go to the police, I will only run away somewhere else. I'll have to start fresh all over again and I'll be worse off than I am now." She brought some tears to her eyes.

Mark and Layla looked at each other.

"Okay, okay," Layla said after a long pause. "We'll leave you be, for now. But when we come to the winter markets next week, we'll give you a decent meal. And take this—" She tipped some coins into Hera's hand. Mark looked at his wife and knew that, despite her apparent surrender, she wasn't done with this young girl yet.

"Besides," Layla said on a lighter note, smiling again, "it's such a wonderful event, and it'd be nice to share it with someone wouldn't it, Mark?" She didn't want to scare the young girl off.

"Yes, it would," Mark said, eager to dispel the tension. "Someone else to decide about colours and materials and about whether various colours 'work' together or not." He leaned across and almost whispered conspiratorially to Hera. "Which I know nothing about but have to spend all day pretending that I do."

"If I'm still around, I'll look out for you," Hera promised, knowing full well she would still be around. A meal would be nice.

Mark suddenly looked at his watch. "Our tram will be here in three minutes, so we need to dash." Layla stayed and fussed a bit more. How could she leave a young girl by herself? But the knowledge that they could miss their tram was enough to drag her away and down the steps.

"We'll come back," she called as she left. They were just in time.

Hera stayed at the cafe and worked her way through the rest of the pastries. A waitress refilled her cup four times during the following hour. Eventually, though, she got up and descended back to the tram station.

She had work to do. The real reason she was living in a tram station in Ducal City.

6

The First Pin Falls

Since the Winter Market's inception eighty-two years ago, it had been the Elder for Security's job to switch on the lights. The task always seemed a bit strange, since the ritual happened in the early afternoon, hours before darkness fell, but that was how it had always been. The ceremony lasted around fifteen minutes, beginning with an anthem played by the Ducal Youth Band and concluding with the flicking of the switch. Sandwiched in the middle was the traditional speech summarising all that had happened in Ducal City the previous year.

As the final notes from the band died away, the Elder for Security took a sip of water from the desk below him and stepped up to the podium. He cleared his throat.

"Ladies and Gentlemen, may I welcome you here today." His voice cracked and he coughed. "This past year has been one of freedom and prosperity for all Anasius. Back in March..." His voice rattled and he tried to clear his throat again, bringing his right hand up to his chest. There were beads of sweat on his forehead, despite the winter chill.

"Back in March...in March..." he tried again, but his voice was fading. He clutched desperately at the podium before swaying and then falling, podium and all crashing to the ground like a rock from the sky.

Within moments, there was a medic at his side and a number of attendants standing around trying to look busy. A minute later, the Mayor of Ducal City got hold of a roving microphone and announced that the Elder for Security was being treated by medical professionals.

"Knowing the Elder's strong sense of duty and commitment to Anasius," the Mayor called, trying to hide his fluster. "He would be horrified if his personal illness disrupted the events of the next few days, so on his behalf, and with the authorisation of the Xcis, I now declare the Winter Market open."

It was perhaps the strangest, darkest opening the market had ever had. But nevertheless, stall owners uncovered their produce, putting the finishing touches to their wares. Entertainers blew into their instruments, checked their gear and made last-minute adjustments to their unicycles and electric bikes. Once they knew the Winter Market was going ahead as planned, the crowd heaved a collective sigh of relief. Many had come on long journeys for this, and whilst they were shocked by what they had just witnessed, they were keen to get on with the festivities. Within minutes, the market was well under way.

Half an hour later, as Hera was looking at the stalls, wondering what to steal for lunch, a voice hailed her.

"We found you!" It was Layla, a beaming smile on her face tinged with relief, and Mark tagging along with her.

"Dreadful to see the Elder for Security taken so sick, wasn't it? And so suddenly, too. Still, I expect he'll be better tomorrow." She began chattering away as before, putting Hera at her ease despite herself.

"Maybe," Hera mumbled, knowing perfectly well that by now, the Elder for Security was in all likelihood dead. "How many stalls are there here?" She changed the subject. She knew that Layla would jump on such a question.

"Oh, hundreds at least. Thousands maybe. There are heaps of stalls selling foods of every kind imaginable, but there are amazing stalls selling craft items and jewellery and paintings and ornaments...Why don't you join us? We've not been here long, and there's masses to see." Layla continued with her mission to look after this stray girl they had met earlier at the tram station.

Hera shook her head.

"It's very kind of you, but I was going to get some food and then head off—"

"—Head off?" Layla couldn't hide her disappointment. "But it's only just begun. We'll get lunch with you. Our favourite stall is on Fifth Street, and they do those venison steaks I told you about." Not taking no for an answer, Layla ignored Hera's hesitation and Hera found herself walking briskly down South Street, her backpack swinging from one shoulder as Layla chatted away happily about her plans for the holidays.

Hera didn't know anything about venison – it wasn't something they had in Turonia. But when she was presented with a plateful of venison steak, mashed sweet potatoes and asparagus, she found to her surprise that Layla was right. It was the most delicious thing she had ever tasted, and hungry as she was, she ate it rather faster than was polite. In fact, she had almost finished before she noticed Mark smiling at her between his slower and more deliberate mouthfuls. She blushed, but Layla laughed.

"Good to see a youngster with a decent appetite," she said.

"I'll say," Mark agreed. "Both our kids have left home now, but I miss having to cook three times as much as we need, only to watch them wolf it down and then ask for more."

Hera decided to be more communicative. It was the least she could do. Besides, she had begun to feel a little curious about the older pair who had taken such an interest in her.

"You have kids?"

Mark smiled.

"Well, Angela is twenty-six and Phil is almost thirty." He looked at Layla. "Seems like only yesterday we were teaching them how to use their implants, and giving them a Scroll..."

Hera looked confused. "Scroll?" she asked. She knew what implants were – she had heard some Seniors talking about them in the cafeteria back in Turonia. Apparently, they were electronic devices fitted into the inner ears to help Anasiuns with their communications. But the "Scroll"? What was that? Some kind of ancient manuscript? And why did children need it?

Mark nodded, stroking his chin as he spoke.

"Yes, the Scroll was written by Xcion the Sovereign..." he trailed off as he saw the deepening confusion on Hera's face. His eyes asked Layla for help

Layla unclipped a little black card from the seam of her cape.

"This is a Scroll," she said, tapping in the corner of the card as Hera watched. The card unfolded itself a few times into something about the size of a piece of A4 paper, with icons flashing in the corner. One looked like an ancient scroll, tied with a ribbon and wax-sealed. Layla tapped the icon. On the screen appeared what seemed to be the first page of a book.

"The Scroll is an ancient book which shows us all about Xcion the Sovereign – His nature, His character and His works. It also contains instructions for life, ethics, ancient prophecies, and how Anasius and our world came into existence."

"Yes," Mark interjected enthusiastically. "It might be ancient, but it's more relevant than anything the academies produce each year. It's the basis of life here in Anasius."

Hera was unimpressed. The country was run based on a book written by primitive people centuries ago? Whatever happened to innovation and progress? It was hardly surprising Anasius was so backward.

Layla noticed her lack of interest and decided it was a conversation to continue another time. She closed the Scroll and clipped it back onto her cloak.

"Anyway, getting our kids their implants was a long time ago, and as for their teenage years...well...the less said about that, the better."

Mark managed to frown and laugh at the same time. "They were pretty decent."

Layla sighed. "Yes, you're right, mostly. But do you remember when Angela turned up with that awful boy from Merksin College, with his shaved head. I still can't understand what she saw in him."

"All she saw was that we'd disapprove."

"Well, he only lasted a few weeks." Layla turned back to Hera again. "Now she's married to a poor, but clever high-school teacher. They love each other, and our first grandchild is on the way, so we're not complaining."

Then she changed tack.

"What about you, Hera? Do you have siblings or cousins or anything?"

Hera remembered little Jethry with his black curly hair and funny giggling laugh, but in that moment, she struggled to fully picture his face. With a jolt she realised her memories of him and of her parents were fading. And Jethry would be eleven by now – maybe she wouldn't even recognise him. There was no way she could tell Layla any of that, so she shook her head.

"No," she lied. "I'm an only child. I was due to start college in a few months, but I guess that won't happen now, will it." She said it as a matter of fact rather than a question.

Mark and Layla remembered her story of her parents being arrested, but they didn't like to ask what for, so

Layla changed the conversation again with a side glance at Mark.

"You know, Hera, we have spare rooms in the house and no-one to feed anymore except ourselves. It's a bit too quiet for my liking. If you're still hunting for somewhere to live, you'd be welcome to stay with us for a bit, just whilst you get yourself organised – we're only two tram stops from here, you know." Her tone was light, but the following pause felt heavy with meaning.

It was a very generous offer. In fact, Mark and Layla had discussed it after their first meeting with Hera on the train ride home. They were convinced Hera was living on the streets. And the weight of concern in Layla's heart hadn't let up since she'd last left Hera in that cafe.

Before Hera could answer, Layla continued, "But you don't need to decide now. Why not come on the rounds with us and explore the market first? There's so much to see. And I have some ideas for the house, but Mark's useless when it comes to decor, so I'd appreciate a bit of help."

Hera made the beginnings of a smile and said, "Well, I guess I could tag along...if you don't mind. Though, I'm better with an axe or with fixing a tram than doing anything with material, to be honest." Layla raised her eyebrows and smiled, carrying on chatting, resting her hand just for a moment on Hera's arm.

But Hera's thoughts were abuzz. The thought of no longer living in the tram station was a tempting one, but she couldn't understand why someone might be so nice to her unless they wanted something from her. What did Mark and Layla want?

A few hours later, following a pleasant day looking at hundreds of market stalls, Hera found herself settling into a little blue bedroom in the attic of a cottage on the edge of Ducal City, with no need any longer to steal her food and lie her way onto trams.

And so it was that Layla and Mark came to harbour an assassin.

7

Elimination Rounds

Under two weeks later, over at Fort Tula, the Elder for Defence was inspecting troops and equipment before descending the hill into Xanver Naval Base. After the Notalian invasion of 316, the fort had been fully refurbished and modernised, and just recently, the installation of new detection and defence equipment had been completed.

Fort Boan on the other side of the bay had been renovated and repurposed as a retreat centre and care home for the elderly. To the north and west, the rooms had views over Mannasa Sound, with Grandy Island looking tantalizingly close just across the water and the northern sea stretching out to the horizon. Rooms to the south looked down over the fields to the naval base and beyond that to Tsarn and Ruscorn Forest. On a clear day, you could see all the way to the southern mountains near the Parlemoni border.

Fort Tula, though, was unapologetically a military base, providing a ready defence of Anasius for the entire northern sea border, with a special focus on River Dagon and the city of Ruwark on its far side. The fort had been rebuilt in 320 after the failed Notalian Invasion, but much more recently it had been given a complete refurbishment once again, bringing the Anasiun defences into the modern era. Miniature sensors and cameras had been installed at regular intervals along the entire length of Carliggan and Ralligan cliffs, both above and below the waterline, as well as around Ruwark's city walls, along the Dagon estuary and, of course, around the naval base itself.

The flagpole at Fort Tula rose majestically from the northwest corner of the whole fort building complex, flying a huge Anasiun standard with its gold eagle and royal crest. The pole itself doubled as a high-powered radio mast, transmitting signals from the operations room below ground to outlying posts across Anasius and, most particularly, to Xcion Strategic High Command over in Arelard Castle.

The Elder for Defence strode along a triple line of perfectly dressed officers in the central quadrangle, taking a moment to have a brief word with a few of them on the way. They were standing stock-still, their heels glued together, their eyes directed straight ahead below the peak of their stiffly starched black caps, with their silver stars glinting in the afternoon sunlight. Their striking red dress uniforms with their gold stripes and silver buckling were accentuated by the impossibly polished black boots. The Captain of the Naval Task Group escorted the Elder for Defence down the line, bringing him finally to Lord Downing, the Admiral of the Fleet, and to Sir Martin Hoye, Armed Services General. Both were in full military regalia for the occasion and greeted the Elder for Defence warmly. They spoke for a few minutes and then Lord Downing led the small party through the huge front doors of the Great Hall and beyond that to the Naval Office, a large high-ceilinged room tastefully decorated in greens and blues. Once their business was complete there, the Elder for Defence was led back out of the Great Hall doors, across the now empty quadrangle and into the armoured cars for the short trip down the hill to the naval base itself.

A large crowd had gathered in front of the academy, waving flags and cheering as the pageantry of the day unfolded both on the large screen on the academy front lawn, and then in real life as the entourage rolled quietly into view to their right. The Elder for Defence stepped from the vehicle into the late afternoon sunshine and waved to the gathered crowd who were pulsing against the fence line. He walked along the line of the crowd for a few dozen metres, shaking hands and exchanging pleasantries with the crowd. At last, he stepped away and strode across to the huge gates which formed the entrance point for Xanver Naval Base. As he moved through the open gates to the guard post beyond, it was the Captain of the Naval Task Group who first noticed that the Elder for Defence was unsteady on his feet. He looked carefully at the Elder's face.

"Are you quite alright, sir?"

The Elder for Defence tried to respond, but his voice seemed to have stopped working. He swayed in a more pronounced way, and Lord Downing reached out to support him. But he was too slow. The Elder for Defence crashed to the floor, jerked once and then never moved again.

“Medic!” the Captain cried as the Elder for Defence fell. “Thankfully, the crowd can no longer see us,” he thought to himself, wondering what on earth was wrong. Lord Downing was already kneeling beside the Elder for Defence, desperately trying to remember all his medical training. He looked for the rise and fall of the Elder’s chest as he felt for a pulse, first on the wrist and then in the neck. But it was no use. The Elder was dead. And moments later, Lord Downing realised his fatal mistake.

“Don’t touch hi…” he began before his own voice failed. He pleaded for help with his eyes, but he knew it was too late. He crumpled to the ground.

The Captain knew what to do.

“Step away!” he commanded to those moving towards the two prone figures. “Whatever this is, it is contagious. Do not touch those men. Seal off this area. Call our hazards team on the emergency line. Paltia?” He looked around for his most senior aide.

“Yes, sir?” The ever-efficient Paltia was just behind the main party.

“Get the palace on the line.”

Suddenly, a calm, sunny evening turned into a hornets’ nest.

*

Three weeks later, Patricia van Olden, the Head of Xcion Strategic High Command (XSHC), was doing her usual job and closing the office down for the night. She had spent the past three weeks ensuring Xanver Naval Base followed all the correct protocols for unknown hazardous substances and stepped up their security as much as possible.

Her head ached. The stress of the death of the Elder for Defence and Lord Downing coupled with all the security revisions she had overseen since had made her very tired. But today, the worst was behind them, and more robust systems were up and running to counter all threats, both domestic and foreign. She had sent her exhausted staff home half an hour ago, and now it was her turn. She pulled the door closed and turned the complex safety key in the lock. She hung it around her neck and made her way down the steps, checking the time as she went. At this rate, perhaps her husband would still be up when she made it home.

She moved across the central hallway with its big curving staircase, and exited through the employee's entrance to the right of the massive oak doors which heralded the entrance to Arelard Castle. As she stepped out into the semi-darkness of the evening, she could hear the river chattering its way out from under the castle and down the rocks in front of her. The sky was clear, the stars were out and there was a distinct chill in the air. She pulled her cape more tightly around her and took a deep breath, striving to forget the stress of the day and to remember the warmth of home. Her two small children would be tucked up in their bunks, and her husband by the fire, waiting for her return.

"Get moving, Patricia" she scolded herself, remembering the time again.

But it was her final thought. Before she had taken one step from the castle, she dropped to the ground like a felled tree. She uttered no sound. There was no change in her expression. If you had been standing nearby, you would have heard the "thump" as her body hit the floor, and the following "thunk" as her head hit the pavement. You would have seen the blood flowing from her temple. But there was no-one nearby. The only witness was someone up in the foothills of Tancon mountain who was watching through a scope. They had spent fifty minutes waiting for this moment. But now, as soon as the Head of XSHC had fallen, the small lone figure in the mountains rose to their feet, packed everything up, slung a long narrow bag across their shoulders and hurried off down a small path towards Beggar's Tarn.

Four hours later, in a little blue attic room in a cottage on the edge of Ducal City, a signal was sent to Turonia via short-wave radio. The third kill mission in Anasius was completed and now the plan was fully under way.

8
Jason and Kia

The relationship had started in earnest when the friends had gathered on the bench at the top of Turner's Hill the way they usually did on a warm evening. This place held a great poignancy. There was something very cathartic about being together here, the place where they had first heard details of Zak's death and of Zika's precarious situation in hospital following their accident on the road those two years ago.

For Zika, it had been a long road of recovery. He was now physically well, but he still struggled with the emotional pain of Zak's passing. His friends had learned that walking, running, sitting and talking all seemed to help. They knew to keep an eye out for him, and they knew the warning signs. It seemed to help him to reminisce about their experiences in Anasius and swap stories. And they considered this place at the top of the hill as a hallowed place to talk about Zak.

On this particular evening, after most of the friends headed off home, Jason and Kia were still deep in conversation. Kia was describing how she felt trying to run XSHC, whilst Jason had been fighting at Ruwark.

As the sky turned pink with the setting sun, their conversation petered out, and they watched in companionable silence as the evening turned to night. It was past 8pm when they left together, and they were holding hands. Neither of them were sure how it happened, but that was four months ago, and they had been inseparable ever since.

Increasingly, though, their closeness kept them away from their other five friends. At first, they had just taken the occasional cinema trip together or visited a local restaurant, but more recently, Marcia had become worried. Their relationship had become intense, and they were distancing themselves from everyone else. She felt that it was an increasingly unhealthy situation, and she didn't know what she could do about it. But when Jason and Kia suddenly announced they were going camping together, she resolved at least to discuss it with the other four.

"It's asking for trouble," she argued as they sat at lunch the next day. "I know we want them to be happy and everything, but I don't think they're thinking straight. Maybe we should invite ourselves along."

"But you hate camping," Joe protested. "And I'm not going. If they want to try and sleep cold and wet on the ground, then let 'em."

"I know," Marcia responded. She looked at her feet, not quite able to articulate how she was feeling

"We're not the relationship police," Joe said. "I don't see what the problem is."

Marcia looked at the others for help, but none of them seemed to want to get involved. She sighed to herself. She hated to see people she cared about making bad decisions, and she was worried.

*

For Kia and Jason, trying to organise their little trip had become problematic. Kia was explaining to Jason how she had gained her parents' permission.

"I just said I wanted to go camping up on the Downs on Saturday night. I told them we'd meet at the top of town in the afternoon and walk up by ourselves, and I asked them to pick me up from the manor car park on Sunday morning. They were fine with it."

Jason grimaced. He had needed to tell his parents there were four of them going, because he knew they'd never let him go just with Kia, and he'd had to buy twice as much food as they'd needed so they were convinced it was okay. It had all been a bit complicated, and he just hoped they didn't see Joe or Marcia's parents, because then there would be a problem. If his parents found out, there'd be no end of trouble.

But somehow, they had made it, and armed with bags of food, they hiked up the hill into the woods. For Kia, watching the sunset was a must, so they put up a tent, got a fire going, and ate snacks whilst they waited. Kia had brought her speaker, so they listened to music, played a bit of cards and complained about the planned end-of-term disco at school.

Later on, as they sat gazing into the fire, Kia gushed about studying law and joining a private firm. She clearly knew a lot about it, and Jason felt out of his depth.

"It sounds great, Kia, but it's not for me. I'm not really certain what lawyers do most of the time. But I know you'll earn a lot," he added.

"I want to be a barrister and work in commercial law," Kia tried to explain. "After my law degree, I'll do another year for the Bar course, and then a year of pupillage in chambers. After that—"

"—But that's five years of study even after you finish your A-levels," Jason interrupted. "Think how much debt you'll have."

"It'll probably be a hundred thousand or so."

Jason blew out his cheeks and shook his head.

"I know," Kia responded. "But once I finish and start work, I could be earning six figures even in my first year..."

Jason gasped. Six figures. He was amazed. He struggled to think much beyond Christmas, let alone beyond the A-levels, university and into his first job. He admired Kia's focus and conviction about what she wanted. He had no idea what he wanted. His dad wanted him to go to university, but he wasn't sure what he'd do even if he did go. He got up and placed another couple of logs onto the dying fire before sitting down again.

"I don't even know if I want to go to uni," he said quietly, staring into the fire.

"That's okay," she said. "You've still got time to figure it out. Technically, applications don't have to be in for another three months. I'll help you."

Jason nodded but he thought to himself, "It seems unlikely that anyone will know what I want to do, when I don't have the faintest clue myself."

The sun had sunk below the horizon now and the night was cold, and Kia was already shivering.

"Let's warm up in the tent."

9

Under Attack

Surprisingly, and completely by accident, it took only an hour for someone to find Patricia's body.

The Head of XSHC was a stickler for security, and never made a mistake. But, for some unknown reason and on this very day, she had failed to pull the employees' door fully shut behind her, so the outer locks did not properly engage. When Arelard security were doing their evening rounds, one of them realised that the employees' door was not fully shut. As he opened the door to then shut it properly, it hit the prone shape of Patricia's dead body. And thus the alarm was raised many hours earlier than had been anticipated. As a result, rather than the usual peaceful slumber, the situation room at Arelard Castle became a hive of activity.

By midnight, key figures in XSHC had gathered in the conference room at Arelard Castle, along with the Director of the Underlord Academy and the Chief of Police, who was pacing the room and muttering quietly to himself. As they waited for the Xcis to arrive, most of them sat or wandered about in virtual silence, unsure what to say, some softly crying, some sitting numbly wondering how on earth this had happened. When Xci1 and Xci2 arrived ten minutes later, directly from Tsarn, Xci1 started proceedings without ceremony.

"Ladies and gentlemen," he said in his deep commanding voice, patting his not insubstantial belly subconsciously as he took a moment to survey the room. "Patricia's death can leave us in no doubt: Anasius is under attack." Unable to say more, he gestured towards the Chief of Police and sat back down.

The Commissioner was a thin wiry man with greying hair immaculately smoothed, and blue piercing eyes. He spoke in a deep gravelly voice, with such clarity and precision that it was immediately obvious why he had been chosen for the job.

"So far, we've lost the Elder for Security to an unknown toxin at the ceremony of the lights at the Ducal Winter Market. We are fairly confident it was administered via the small bottle of water from which he sipped immediately prior to giving his speech, but whilst the bottle is clearly visible on camera *before* his fall, it disappeared as the crowds thronged through the area.

"Then, three weeks ago, the Elder for Defence was also killed by an unknown toxin on an official tour at Xanver Naval Base. In trying to come to his aid, Lord Downing, Admiral of the Fleet, was exposed to the same toxin and died two minutes later. Security protocols have been upgraded.

"And now," the Commissioner's eyes flicked up to the clock to check the time. "Just three hours ago, Patricia van Olden, our own Head of this XSHC, was also killed. Initial investigation suggests that she was shot by a long-range rifle on the steps of Arelard Castle as she left for home – a fact that is yet to be confirmed but seems most likely."

There were a few gasps around the room as his words hit home. A rifle? Such a thing had not happened for centuries. The 300-year-old All-nations Arms Agreement, which outlawed the production and use of any firearms in any nation throughout the sub-continent, had ensured it.

"This means that, if our initial inquiries prove true, someone has deployed a long-range rifle for assassination, and our hand is forced. Xci2?"

Xci2 nodded and took up the narrative in his softer lilting voice with its distinct southern twang. He was a slightly taller man than Xci1, and his slender frame made him appear taller still. "Thank you, Commissioner. Yes, if the cause of death for Patricia is verified, it will be incumbent upon us to inform all the other nations in the southern continent of the presence and use of a firearm on our soil. Many nations will wish to increase their surveillance and security protocols as a result, especially at their borders. As for us, we are raising our military alert level from Delta 4 to Delta 3. The assassination of two senior Elders and now the Head of this XSHC leaves us in no doubt. Make no mistake, Anasiuns, the threat of attack has become a reality." There were looks of horror, disgust, anger and fear in different measure on the faces of the gathered company.

"The key now is to plan the way forward. First, we need to know who our enemy is – who is striking at the heart of our security and government, and what is their eventual goal? Second, how do we raise the alert to Delta 3 without causing panic amongst our people?"

There were nods of agreement around the room.

Glancing across at his brother, Xci1 ran his fingers through his fast-greying hair and spoke again. "The Royals want personal security to be provided for all Elders as they conduct their regular business, and any non essential public appearances will be suspended. Commissioner, I am assuming your security forces can arrange this?"

The Commissioner nodded his agreement but added, "I think it would be wise to buttress the security for Your Highnesses, too. As our overall leaders, the Xcis may be targeted."

Xci2 frowned, not wanting to cause a fuss. Xci1 paused and thought for a moment before acquiescing with a nod. "And to further increase our security at this time, we would like to install Chines as interim Head of XSHC."

Chines, a moustached man in his mid-thirties, stood up.

"As the second in command for three years," Xci1 continued, "Chines has a better understanding of the job than virtually anybody else, so he will move into that role with immediate effect."

Chines coughed before speaking. His hands were sweaty.

"Of course, Your Highness. Err...I am willing to help in any way I can." He drew another shaky breath. "However, since I fall far short of Patricia's thirty years of experience,

I will need all the help I can get. In the next few weeks, we're going to have to work longer and harder than most of us have ever worked. There is imminent danger to the national security of Anasius, and it is up to us to put a stop to it."

"Exactly," Xci1 agreed with a slight smile. He always seemed to know precisely what to do. "And this is why we're creating a new investigative taskforce under the XSHC's direction, selected by Chines and his team. They will launch a full-scale forensic investigation into all three assassinations and conduct detailed security assessments, examination of video footage and on-the-ground searches. They will also profile any individual who is found to be in more than one of those locations within twelve hours of the assassinations. We will find the location from which that rifle shot was fired, too, and conduct a detailed forensic examination of the site in hope of finding the shooter." He paused, wiping the sweat from his forehead, and then said, "Any questions about our strategy moving forward?"

There was a moment's silence as some of the best brains in the country mulled over his words, and those of the Commissioner before him.

A castle aide working for the security team commented, "What are we going to tell the people about Patricia's death?"

"Well, we must not lie to our people, of course," Chines responded with uncharacteristic conviction. "But we are also keen to keep the peace. We will say that she died in the line of duty, and request privacy at this difficult time. Anything else?"

A younger, athletic-looking man with a fast-receding hairline and large sideburns spoke up. "Your Highness," he said, looking worried. "Your Highness Xci1, may I speak to you in private?" He swallowed and glanced about. He realised it was a bold request.

Xci1 furrowed his brow. Then his face softened a little.

"Of course," he said. With one last nod to the gathered people, Xci1 dismissed the room, watching as they filtered out, a new seriousness now resting on all their faces. Xci2 left last, but not unwillingly – he had a good deal to oversee. Then the athletic man approached Xci1, and they met at a corner desk.

"Don't you think it would be worth inviting the wider security fraternity to a meeting to brainstorm the way ahead? Things are getting pretty desperate, and someone may have an idea we have not yet considered."

Xci1 sighed. Then, after a few moments' thought, he nodded in agreement. "You may be right." Such a drastic measure hadn't been taken for years, but the man was right, things were desperate. "But I do not wish to alert everyone to our concerns at this stage. If we summon the senior security network, news will get out to the general public. It may be that we need to do it anyway, but not yet. So yes, get everything together to send a summons, but do not send it until I give the go-ahead. Are you happy with that?"

"Absolutely Sire, of course, Your Highness." The man looked visibly relieved. "Consider it done."

10

Life-Changing

Six weeks later, Kia knew she had a major predicament.

She was top of every class at school. She was heading for top grades. She was working towards university and law school and becoming a barrister. She had well-to-do parents who were always keen to be seen doing the right thing. They moved in circles of affluence, took foreign holidays, played tennis and golf and generally fitted in with the wealthy elite, even though they sent Kia to a state school – "to teach her how the real world works," they would say. Kia was the model child, the hard-working and high-achieving kid who makes it hard for others to compete. Most of them didn't try to.

But now she had a problem. The complicated, turn-your-world-upside-down, mess-up-your-life kind of problem. For about the first time in her life, she had absolutely no idea what to do. Nor did she know who she could actually talk to about it. She should talk to Jason, but that seemed far too difficult. She should talk to her parents, but that seemed even worse. Eventually, she made an urgent appointment with the school counsellor for the next day. Then she wished she hadn't. She couldn't eat. She couldn't think straight. She couldn't sleep.

Before the appointment, she had to endure tutor group and then a whole history lesson. She got through tutor time somehow, but history was a blur. She couldn't remember who Richard III was, even though they'd been studying him for the last three lessons, and she couldn't even remember the time period. Mr Craddock was concerned. Kia was his best and brightest student, and she was getting the most basic things wrong today. Something was up. He mentioned it to her tutor during morning break. By then, Kia was crying in the counsellor's office.

She hadn't meant to cry. She hadn't really meant to attend the appointment. But now the cat was out of the bag. The counsellor was very sweet, and booked Kia into a clinic for Monday morning – four days away. She urged Kia to speak to her parents, but Kia shook her head. The counsellor was adamant she should tell someone – someone who could be with her through the procedure and look after her afterwards, preferably an adult. But the only people Kia could think of speaking to were Marcia and Jason, and Jason was definitely a distant second. So she was crying. Was she doing the right thing? She really didn't know. But she knew that anything else would be devastating for her future, and that she definitely did not want. She spent a full hour with the counsellor, missing her German lesson entirely.

At lunch, she managed to get Marcia alone to talk. She took a while getting around to it, but Marcia guessed before she needed to actually say it.

"Jason?" asked Marcia.

Kia just nodded. She couldn't speak anymore. Her eyes glistened. She was determined not to cry, but the lump was well and truly in her throat. She swallowed.

"Have you told him?" Marcia probed.

Kia shook her head. How could she? What would be the point?

"You must tell him," Marcia insisted. "He has a right to know."

Kia swallowed again. "Why? It's my body, not his."

Marcia looked at her. "Because now it's not only your body, is it." It was a statement, not a question. "And this situation you find yourself in – it's his fault just as much as it is yours. He needs to know."

Kia was shaking her head again. "No, I can't. What... what if he wants to keep it? I...I can't put that pressure on him," she blurted.

Marcia's response was immediate. "You can't put the pressure of *not* telling him on yourself. You are both responsible for this, so you need to *both* figure out what to do."

Kia shook her head again. She didn't tell Marcia that she'd already decided.

Marcia was worried. Worried Kia wouldn't tell Jason. Worried Kia would do something she would regret. Worried about what would happen if Kia didn't do something she would regret. The consequences and confusions. And she felt annoyed with herself. How had she allowed it to get to this? But the following day, Friday, Kia decided to tell Jason as they walked home together. It was not an easy conversation.

11

A New Mission

Hera could not understand why anyone would let their lives be disrupted by an unknown homeless teenager, let alone an older couple living a quiet and enjoyable life. Mark and Layla got nothing out of having her stay except higher bills and more work to do. So she had committed herself to taking on the lion's share of the housework, leaving only the cooking to Mark. He strangely enjoyed it.

Hera opened her eyes and knew without looking at the clock that it was 5am exactly. She had been trained that way, of course, and no amount of lying in bed and trying to get back to sleep was ever going to undo that training. She rolled out of bed and got ready for a workout. Within a couple of minutes, she was training as she always did – one-hundred press-ups, eighty squats, and a plank for at least two minutes. Today, though, she was interrupted by a quiet buzz on her short-wave radio.

She removed it from its hiding place in an alcove behind the wardrobe, adjusted the left-hand dial and listened. The voice came again.

"Call-sign O-O-D-8, this is the Eagle's Nest, signifier DFXX2."

Hera depressed the yellow button and spoke as loudly as she dared. "O-O-D-8 to Eagle's Nest, signifier K99EJ," she panted. She let go of the button and waited.

There was a short burst of static, and then she heard, "Elder for Transport, two weeks. Copy?"

She pushed the yellow button again. "Copy, Elder for Transport, two weeks."

"Out."

"Out."

Suddenly, two days after Patricia Van Olden was killed, Hera had a new mission.

She crossed the little room to her desk and sat down, turning to the small picture of Ruscorn Forest that hung from the blue wall. She pulled out the keyboard which hung below the desk and began tapping at the keys. She knew this would be quieter than using the more common voice-activation method. As soon as she started, the Ruscorn Forest picture expanded to twice its size, faded out and became what looked like an ordinary computer monitor. Images were already flashing in response to Hera's work on the keys. Within moments, she was lost in her research.

Over the next three days, she spent a long time at the screen. She learned a good deal about the Elder for Transport. He had been in post for over three years, and, in fact, he had served four years as an Elder as well. He was an experienced politician. She learned the names of his wife and two sons, his medical history, his identity details, his net worth, his business enterprises, and so on. She hacked into his diary, explored his movements and established his habits and the things he loved. She discovered he lived a fairly regimented life, rising early and retiring to bed early every day. Learning this, she smiled broadly. It had just made her job so much easier. She spent four hours poring over the blueprints and satellite images of his house and grounds. She spent a few more hours examining his home security system and digging into the lives and backgrounds of the four men who formed his security detail. The more she studied, the more an idea began to form in her mind.

*

Ten days after that, Hera awoke at 2am, pulled on her camouflage clothing and slipped from Mark and Layla's cottage without making a sound. She began a fast-paced jog; she had a long way to go if she was to be properly positioned before dawn. She crossed the main road and ran north towards the junction on the road out of the city, keeping a sharp ear out for any traffic. There was none, but she knew that shortly there would be – the truck heading off to the market in Tsarn would leave the depot in Ducal City sometime around 2:30am.

As it turned out, the truck was late. For Hera, who was virtually invisible in her camouflage kit as she lay prone in the roadside ditch, it seemed like an age, and she wondered whether or not she had missed it. If she didn't catch the truck, her visit to the home of the Elder for Transport would be stopped before it had even started.

Finally, though, she heard the unmistakable whine of the electric truck as it headed her way. The driver slowed for the junction, which Hera had counted upon, but it slowed far less than she expected. She had to run and jump in order to catch the back handle and swing herself onto the rear of the truck. With the items she was carrying, this was a difficult manoeuvre, and she nearly dropped one of her packages in the process. But, somehow, she managed to grasp the truck handle with one hand, grip her parcel with the other and keep her backpack secured on her back as the truck accelerated away alarmingly from the junction. In moments, she was on her way to Tsarn.

Sitting on the truck, her thoughts whirled. She had completed a number of missions like this before, but she still thrilled at the prospect. Her green eyes sparkled. The sneaking around, the high stakes, the satisfaction of a job well done...it was electric. But, as the engine whined around her and the road whizzed by, something else slithered into her mind, something cold. Doubt? She pushed it away and straightened her back. "Focus on the mission," she told herself. "The mission is all that matters" – the Black Ops mantra rang in her head.

She glanced behind her. If another vehicle approached the truck from behind, she would be spotted in a moment, and she hated that this part of her plan depended almost entirely on luck. She knew it was unusual for any vehicles to travel the road before 4am, but it was not unheard of – she just had to hold on and hope.

Her luck held, and half an hour later, as the truck approached Tsarn, she knew the time had nearly arrived for her to disembark. The truck slowed towards the city, and she launched her backpack towards the verge, closely followed by the package. Next, gathering herself together as best she could, she leapt from the truck. She was aiming for the ditch, but she had underestimated the speed of the truck and landed awkwardly. She went straight into a forward roll over into the ditch itself, coming to a juddering halt on a wet clump of weeds, panting, bruised but otherwise unharmed.

Retrieving her package and backpack, she crossed the road and ran up the hillside into some low trees and bushes. As soon as she was shielded from view, she stopped and examined the package carefully, looking for damage, however minor. Whilst the outer wrapping of the flat package had some scratches and a tear in it, when she unwrapped it and checked it over, the item itself remained pristine. "What a relief," she thought, rewrapping it.

Next, she inspected the backpack. It had sustained significant damage from hitting the tarmac and bouncing into the ditch, but it was holding together. When she opened it up, most of the contents seemed unaffected, aside from a package of cookies she had brought at the last minute – they had taken the brunt of the impact. Incredibly, the small glass vials she had brought were unbroken. Sighing in relief, she repacked the backpack, slung it over her shoulders, picked up the package and began a forty-minute jog through the woods in the direction of Tsarn.

Despite her navigational skills and having spent hour after hour poring over the satellite images, it still took her some time to locate her destination. Only through her night-vision goggles could she see through the darkness – the sky was clouded, but it was a new moon. She had selected this day for that very reason. She emerged from the brush, moved cautiously across the rough grass and arrived at the rear fence of the the Elder for Transport's property – distinctive not just because it was a solid metal structure, but also because of the discreet but noticeable barbed wire that looped around its top. She checked her watch: 5:15am. She had under thirty minutes to organise herself and execute the mission. The Elder for Transport would emerge for his morning swim at 5:45am, fifteen minutes after the sky began to lighten in the pre-dawn. She located the huge oak on the edge of the property with its large branch protruding over the fence. It was her best option for gaining entry.

In her backpack were two diving weights, a tiny, motorised drill, a small pot and brush, two tiny vials, a hypodermic, a small canister, a little sponge, a rubberised facemask, a short hose, an oxygen cannister, and some small folding steps. She removed the night-vision goggles from her face and dropped them on the grass. Then she changed out of her camouflage gear and into the full-body black wetsuit and hood which had been stuffed into the front pocket of her backpack. She pulled out some folding steps and opened them beneath the branch. Picking up the flat package, she unwrapped it and put her arms through its thin straps, and then refitted her rucksack over the top.

It is very difficult to make an accurate estimate of vertical height from a satellite photo, and as she climbed up the two steps and looked up, she knew she had considerably underestimated the height of the branch. She crouched and then sprang for it anyway, driving her feet into the steps and stretching upwards. Her hands scrabbled to get a hold but failed, and she fell in an ungainly heap beside the steps. It took two more attempts before she finally hooked her hands over the branch, swung herself out and got her right leg over it as well. The ground seemed alarmingly far away, but she ignored this fact – there would be plenty of time to think it over later. Now was the time for action.

Heart beating fast, she stared through the thin foliage, over the fence and to the house at the opposite end of an immaculately kept garden. The night was dark, so she knew her chances of detection at this point were slim, but the floodlights lit the pathway which ran along the back wall of the house and a good deal of the lawn nearer to her as well. She saw the guard almost immediately. He was wearing black combat gear with a baton swinging lazily from one hand and a taser clipped to his belt. He looked rather bored walking along the path by the house. He turned at the far end and disappeared around the corner. She breathed again. From her detailed analysis in her bedroom, she knew she had about five minutes before the second guard appeared at the opposite end of the building.

Catlike, she climbed along the branch to the trunk of the tree and made her descent to the garden. A few minutes of clambering later, she was crouched beside a beautifully manicured bush in the shape of a large dome, looking towards the swimming pool. She checked her watch for the umpteenth time. Ninety seconds to go before the next guard would appear.

She removed her boots, pushing them deeply beneath the bush. Then she unfolded the flat package and locked all the sides into place. Now it formed a long, low box with one of the largest two faces missing. The inside was coloured a dusky forest green, but in high contrast, the outside was sky blue with darker lines across it dividing it into squares. Next, she removed the items she needed - the oxygen cannister, short hose and weights - from her backpack, before pushing it under the bush. After that, she pulled the diving mask from her left pocket and connected it to the cannister of oxygen using the thin tube. Fitting the mask to her face, she picked up the oxygen tank in one hand, stooped to grasp the box and the weights with the other hand and ran to the pool, checking her watch as she ran. Less than thirty seconds to go.

She slipped as quietly as she could into the pool at its deepest point, taking the box upside down with her. Then she swam rapidly down to the bottom directly under the lip of a diving board. Using the weights to help her, she lay down on the bottom of the pool and then pulled the box over her head, breathing through the mask, the air bubbles collecting under the box. As the darkness began to give way to a grey pre-dawn, the box at the bottom of the pool blended almost perfectly with the blue tile pattern which covered the pool's base, rendering it virtually invisible. Later, as the early morning light grew, it would be impossible to see, even if you knew what to look for.

Hera was in position only seconds before the second guard appeared above her, walking calmly along the paved walkway next to the house. It took him ninety seconds to traverse the side of the house and then he, like the first guard, disappeared around the corner.

In the pool, Hera was watching the seconds on her watch, desperately keeping count. She had no way of knowing whether the guard was on time, and she had no way of knowing if his walk had taken more or less time than usual. So she had to rely entirely upon all the work she had done over the past few days analysing the pattern of guard movements. The guard had been gone for nearly a full minute before Hera deemed it safe and emerged from the pool, checking the walkway as soon as it was in view. Seeing it empty, she breathed out in relief.

And now she knew she had at least twenty minutes, because the guards had a rest break in the guard house at the front of the property before setting off on their rounds again. She slipped out from under the box and swam to the surface. Climbing from the pool, she ran to the bush, retrieved her rucksack and ran back to the poolside. There, she took the drill and slithered along the diving board until she was within a foot of the end, dangling above the water at the deep end of the pool. She selected a point a few centimetres from the end and bored a small hole almost all the way through. Whilst the drill operated silently, the board vibrated and hummed as she worked, and she was terrified someone was going to hear it.

Nobody did. She returned to her rucksack, retrieved a few more items and slithered back along the diving board to the hole. She removed the dust using a little brush, collecting all the particles in the pot she had brought. She placed one of the vials and the spring-loaded hypodermic into the hole and realised she had been slightly overgenerous in her drilling. She poured a little of the debris back into the hole and tried again. This time, as she pushed the vial down and put the hypodermic in place, the needle protruded about half a centimetre. She covered the vial and then the needle with debris until it was level with the surface once more. Then she poured the epoxy from another canister into the hole. It soaked in quickly, and from her experiments at the workshop in Ducal City, she knew it would be perfectly dry in twenty minutes. The spike was set. She slithered back to the poolside to return the gear to her backpack. She dried the side of the pool using the towel she had brought, slid a pair of pliers under the diving board where they would not be noticed until she needed them and then returned her rucksack to the bush. She checked her watch again and her eyes widened. A guard could appear at any moment. She flew back to the pool and slipped into the water, diving swiftly back to her hiding place under the box.

Seconds later, a guard appeared at the far corner and made his way down the walkway. A minute after that, on the dot of 5:45 as always, the patio doors on the side of the house slid open and the Elder for Transport stepped out into the cold morning. He nodded an absent "good morning" to the guard, who tipped his cap in return. The Elder had a good deal to do today and his thoughts were on the Xci's meeting in City Hall at noon. He was wondering how to break it to them that the new transport hub in Ruwark was going to go considerably over budget. He put the virtually empty coffee cup onto the patio table, removed the towel from his waist and folded it over the railing as he always did. Then he mounted the diving board.

As he jumped, he felt the needle prick his foot and his eyes widened both in pain and in surprise. But, already in motion, he dived, hitting the water with minimal splash. Under the box at the deep end, Hera's heart bashed against her chest as she felt the shockwave of the Elder for Transport's dive.

The Elder swam lengths in his usual fashion. Today, however, he felt more tired than usual, sluggish. As he left the deep end for his third length, he realised he was in trouble. His limbs were lead, and he was struggling to keep his head above water. Within moments, his arms could no longer move. Hera felt his movement stop and knew she had been successful. She emerged from her hiding place at the bottom of the pool and pushed the box and weights out onto the poolside before hauling herself out. As the Elder for Transport went limp in the pool behind her, Hera climbed back onto the diving board. Using the pliers she had stowed away, she snipped off the needle from the hypodermic, before pushing carefully on the drying epoxy mixture until the syringe was covered. In another ten minutes, the epoxy would harden completely, and no-one would have any idea there was a vial and hypodermic hidden within it. The tiny prick on the underside of his foot would be invisible even to a trained pathologist, and he would have no need to hunt for it anyway – Hera had made sure of that.

She collected the second glass vial from her rucksack and tipped the contents into the dregs of coffee at the bottom of the Elder's coffee cup. The most likely conclusion would be suicide.

Moments later, Hera was on the other side of the fence, stripping off the wetsuit, drying herself quickly and donning the camouflage gear once again. Checking she had left nothing behind, she broke into a run across the scrub and into the woods beyond and out towards the edge of town.

She hitched a lift back to Ducal City, walked to Mark and Layla's home and made a discreet entry via her bedroom window. Changing into her night clothes, she emerged, rubbing her head and asking for painkillers.

The unexplained death of the Elder for Transport, discovered floating in his pool early that morning, dominated the news that day.

12

A Cry for Help

The next morning, Chines was at his desk in XSHC. His shoulders were slumped, his eyes were hollow and he stared unseeing at the piece of paper in front of him. He had done everything he could think of to try to protect senior Anasiun leaders – the Xcis, the Elders and senior security personnel. He had called each one individually, urging them to take precautions. He had constructed a list which had formed a central part of his communication with all of them. He'd even drafted in retired officers to supply extra cover.

"Keep your eyes and ears open and your wits about you. Take note of anything out of the ordinary and report it immediately."

"Don't go out in the dark unless you are accompanied by at least two security officers."

"Make sure we know about your plans here at XSHC – keep us informed of changes to your plans."

"We will upgrade the physical security at your property – cameras, motion detectors, smoke alarms, fences and gates."

"If you have a strict routine, vary it as much as possible."

Most had followed the list, albeit complaining about limits to their freedom. But the Elder for Transport was a military man. He could take care of himself, he'd argued, assuring Chines that his own personal security detail was quite up to the task. And as for, "if you have a strict routine, vary it as much as possible," well that was like telling a racing driver to stay out of cars.

This highlighted Chines' problem. He did not have the authority to enforce any of his recommendations. All he could do was advise and supply help where help was wanted. And so the Elder for Transport had been killed.

Chines sighed and put a hand to his throbbing temple. Since Patricia had gone, he had worked with more intensity and drive than he had ever worked in his life. He had done everything he could think of doing. And *still* this assassin had carried out their work. He had failed.

With that thought, he picked up his pen and began to write on the paper in front of him. Xci1 had called an emergency meeting for that afternoon, and Chines had decided to hand in his resignation letter. It was the only decent thing to do.

*

As soon as he heard the news about the Elder for Transport, Xci1 instructed the athletic man with sideburns to send the summons to the senior security network. By lunchtime, virtually all senior and middle-managing security personnel had received orders to meet in the ballroom at Arelard Castle that very afternoon. Many were irritated that their plans for the day had been thrown into disarray. Some were flustered. But, despite the cheery conversations and surface chats en route, all were worried – a call to an emergency meeting was extremely rare. Something major was happening.

As they arrived that warm afternoon, they were security-checked, scanned and provided with a security card – a precaution they had not experienced since terrorist threats were made on their country ten years previously. They were hushed and grim-faced as they moved almost silently into the castle.

It occurred to some of them that the grand ballroom with its white-panelled ceiling and dark oak floor would be far too big a room for a meeting of this size, but since the smaller conference room was being refurbished, it would have to do. The plush, deep red curtains lined the narrow windows like sentries, the grate in the huge fireplace was austerely empty, and the men and women in the oil paintings seemed to frown down at them. Scattered along the edges of the room were ten circular tables, each dressed with a white cloth, pens and cards, three monitors and a large number rising from its centre on a thin metal rod. At the far end of the room, both Xci1 and Xci2 were seated on the dais, and there were sixty chairs set out in rows before the dais, awaiting everyone. As soon as the security personnel realised they were in the presence of royalty, they congregated quietly and obediently, filling up the chairs with a soft rustling and occasional whispered "Excuse me".

The Arelard official just inside the ballroom door was looking at the large black musical instrument to the right of the stage. As he stood there, he reminisced about the summer concerts they had enjoyed here only a month ago. So much had changed.

Xci1 rose to his feet and moved to the podium with solemnity.

"Ladies and Gentlemen," he began, touching his forehead in the Anasiun custom. "Anasius is under attack. The Elders for Security and for Defence have been murdered, along with Lord Downing and Patricia van Olden, the Head of XSHC." As he spoke, there was a rising murmur from the group – some of them were still under the impression that those good people had died of sickness or by accident.

"And now, just this morning, the Elder for Transport was killed at his home on the edge of Tsarn. There is clearly a cunning and ruthless assassin working in Anasius, who is seeking out influential people and taking them out." Xci1 began to pace the stage, his brow furrowing and his hand subconsciously rubbing his stomach. Although he had moved away from the microphone, his deep voice carried effortlessly to the gathered people. "The events of today have meant we felt it necessary to widen the net and bring all of you into the conversation. We have brought you here for a brainstorming exercise. Xci2 will explain whilst I move to XSHC."

He nodded to Xci2 and exited via a side door, his greying hair not quite as slicked back as usual. He headed towards the situation room, whilst Xci2 strode to the podium.

"We are doing virtually everything we can think of," Xci2 said, much less brusquely, but no less seriously. "XSHC and a team from the national police force have been investigating the murders for the last two weeks, and we have increased security for senior figures in the country. Clearly, though, this is not enough. We need your ideas about how we can proceed."

He then divided them into ten groups and instructed them to work together to think of ways that would detain this assassin, expose their handler and discover their wider purpose. To help the groups, they had been given the details of the current investigation which could be found in the XSHC folder on the screens at the tables. And they were to update XSHC via their Scroll every thirty minutes.

"If you have an urgent idea," Xci2 called above the growing din as the groups began, "please inform me directly. I'll be working right here this afternoon." He pointed across to a large desk which stood just off the dais to the right.

After thirty minutes of this, an older gentleman who must have been at least in his seventies was moving uncertainly towards Xci2. How did one approach a Royal? He couldn't remember. Xci2 heard him coming and looked across. The gentlemen coughed and gave half a bow.

"Your Highness," he began. "I am just wondering whether the Xcis have called for help? There's no mention of it in the folder..."

"Called for help?" Xci2 said. "We've called all sixty of you."

The gentleman blushed.

"Yes, Your Highness," he paused. "I mean, I know that. It's just....well, you know, like at the Summer Palace?"

Xci2 looked again at the man in front of him. His back was stooped, his clothes ancient and his hand tremored. Xci2 sighed. He didn't have time for this.

"Oh dear," the older man apologised, "I fear I am doing this very badly. Let me try to explain."

"That would be a good idea," Xci2 thought, but refrained from saying it aloud.

"When Notalia invaded us back in 316, Xci1 made a royal call for help, and eight teenagers from another world came and helped us defeat them. And when the Royals were murdered at the Summer Palace in 381, Prince Arlon made a royal call for help, and seven teenagers from another world came and helped to put Anasius back on track..."

Suddenly, Xci2 understood. It was obvious. The history came flooding back to him. He felt a wave of regret for underestimating the man.

"We should call for help again?" he said.

"Yes, Your Majesty. It seems to me that Anasius needs all the help it can get," the older man nodded. "There's no guarantee anyone will come, of course, but it might be worth a try..."

"You're right," Xci2 reassured him, putting a hand on the man's bony shoulder. "Thank you for being bold, I will ask Xci1 to get onto it right away." He paused, and then said, "I'm sorry I did not catch your name?"

The gentleman grew red again.

“Oh, my name is Gutchins. I’m just a clerk for the Mayor’s office.” Then he couldn’t help adding, “I’ve worked there fifty-seven years.”

Xci2 smiled.

“And we are so grateful for your long service. Let’s keep this idea of calling for help to ourselves for the moment, Gutchins. We don’t want to raise expectations only to have them dashed again. What do you think?”

The idea that a Xci might be seeking his opinion was so far from Gutchins’ expectations that he froze. All he could think of to say was, “Well…I, I think you are very wise, Your Highness.”

Xci2 thanked him again and watched as Gutchins bowed and shuffled back to his table. He turned back to the screen on his desk and fired a rapid message to Xci1.

The royal call for help went out ten minutes later.

13
The Party

The Christmas party was full of laughter. A bunch of teenagers sat together under white and silver strung lights in the Partridge family home. There was a huge tree in the lounge decorated entirely in silver and an open fire roared in the grate.

Tim, the youth leader, welcomed everyone, thanked the Partridge family for their hospitality and got things going with an opening game. It was called "stoop" and it involved trying to pick up a cereal box from the floor using only your teeth, and without touching the floor except with your feet. It took quite some time and much laughter – especially when one of the boys, Jackson, bent over and split his trousers.

Jason and Kia joined in, managing to laugh along with everyone else, but their hearts were not in it. They had not said much since their walk home the evening before when Jason had agreed with Kia's decision about what to do about the pregnancy. Jason was uneasy about it, but the magnitude of what it meant felt too overwhelming to comprehend. And besides, he felt it should be Kia's decision not his, so he resolved to support her in it. As he gazed across at her, he wondered what was going through her mind. In the last day, so much had changed.

After the game, they were invited to the kitchen to collect food. The kitchen island was packed. There were roasting tins piled with steaming turkey and ham and crackling. There were dishes filled with pigs in blankets and roast potatoes and new potatoes and carrots and peas and sweetcorn and green beans and red cabbage and sprouts. There were jugs of gravy and plates of stuffing balls and jars of sauces. It was a feast. The hungry teenagers filled their plates amidst the sound of happy chatter, and then went through to the dining room which was sparkling with decorations.

Boughs of fir and holly lined the mantelpiece, candles flickered in the fireplace and a smaller Christmas tree twinkled on the dresser. Somehow, the Partridges had managed to put enough tables together to make room for everyone – tables covered in thick white cloths and sprinkled with tiny silver stars, jellybeans, silver crackers and yet more candles. The young people got themselves seated, and the hum of chatter faded away as they got down to the serious business of eating. For Kia, who loved her food, eating was no longer an appealing option. She picked at her food with her fork, hoping no-one would notice her discomfort. A little later, various friends got up to go and refill their plates or glasses, and in the midst of this Kia took her plate, left it discretely on the side in the kitchen and hunted for a bathroom. When she returned ten minutes later, she found herself some water and sat down at her place at the table.

As Jason worked his way through his second full plate, he was watching Kia. She hadn't eaten anything.

"Kia, are you finished?" Mrs Partridge asked from the doorway.

"Yes, thank you," Kia responded, putting a smile on her face. "I'm not sure I could eat any more if I wanted to."

It was taken the way she had hoped it would be.

"Well, I may be able to tempt you. Any moment now we'll bring dessert out. You won't want to miss that." Mrs Partridge bustled about, filling glasses, offering more meat.

"You're very kind," Kia responded, "But I'm really not sure I could eat anything else; I'll make myself sick."

"Clever response," Jason admired for the hundredth time. He was fairly sure she had been sick already.

After the meal, they returned to the lounge where Tim gave the Christmas talk. He began by reading excerpts from the Bible. He spoke of Mary, a teenage girl who found herself pregnant and unmarried – a situation of much shame in the ancient world. Jason and Kia gave each other subtle but furtive glances as he spoke. Tim described Mary's visit to her cousin Elizabeth, who, despite being elderly, was also expecting. When Mary arrived, the baby in Elizabeth's womb "leapt for joy." And later, the shepherds visited the baby Jesus in the manger. After that, Jason didn't really listen to much of Tim's talk, because something had struck him with great force. He felt the hairs on his arm stand on end. Jesus had been described as a baby, but so had what was inside Elizabeth's womb. Not just an "it" or a "thing" or a "bundle of cells" or a "potential baby" as he'd heard so many times before. No, that too, the Bible said, was a *baby*.

And in that moment, with the force of it hitting him in the stomach, Jason realised what he had really known all along. There was a baby in Kia's womb. A person. As the idea washed over him, he felt sick. He immediately wanted to talk to Kia, but she left the party early, straight after Tim's talk.

Jason texted her later that evening, trying to explain what he had realised. But her responses became progressively angry: "But it's inside of me, Jas," she said. "It's my body." And "It's not your decision to make," and "It's all very well for you to say, you're a guy." He was increasingly sorry for her distress, but he couldn't shake off the awful feeling in the pit of his stomach. He could feel his emotions flowing into his phone, making his texts strong and rushed.

When the last text came in from Kia, telling him to "Leave off," there was a lump in his throat. He knew they had made an awful mistake. And now he was powerless to do anything other than watch as Kia turned an awful mistake into something far worse. He sat at his desk. He paced his room. He had no idea what to do.

After a fretful night, Jason was not able to see Kia in the morning because his parents had insisted on going to church. They only ever went to church at Christmas and Easter, but they had decided this year that they would attend a carol service on the Sunday morning *before* Christmas. So it was not until they had finished eating lunch that Jason could finally organise himself to go and see Kia as he usually did on a Sunday. He pulled his phone from his pocket and started typing a message.

But before he could finish it, a jolt surged through him, his body flickered and glitched, and he disappeared, his phone clattering to the ground behind him. Jason had been extracted.

14
Eavesdropping

Jason tried to get his bearings. Being extracted was always confusing, not just because he didn't know when it was going to happen, but because he never had any idea where he had been extracted to. The chair on which Jason had been sitting had now become a small fruit crate and he found himself squashed beneath a long wide table over a hard cobblestone street. His legs already ached.

The air was full of noise, and all kinds of conversations were going on around him. Talking, bartering, the clattering of tables, a baby crying...The sound cut through him and sapped his concentration. He shook his head to clear it. He could smell damp hessian and animals and cut flowers and barbecue food. His stomach growled. Someone was busking cheerfully and a little off key. Others were shouting, debating prices, all in an accent he recognised but could not quite place. Clearly, he was in a marketplace somewhere. Thankfully, he had the presence of mind to stay still for a few moments to try and figure out where he was.

There was a big piece of canvas across the front of the table, which prevented him from seeing out onto the roadway, but he was hemmed in by boxes and sacks, making it an excellent hiding place. The only problem was that it was very cramped, and whilst a seven-year-old would have found it ideal, six-foot-tall Jason had to fold himself up to avoid hitting his head. Before he began to push a few boxes aside and move out, the next conversation gave him pause.

"...the greatest city in the country, if not in the whole Western continent."

"I know, right? A new subway system. A new city hall. The athletics stadium opening next week. The mall over on Fourth Street. Crask is burgeoning."

Jason drew his breath in sharply, his heart beginning to race. Could it be?

"I know some folks are unhappy about the way the NLA is run nowadays, but the Royals are right. It's definitely working."

The voices were interrupted by a much harsher noise just a few feet from Jason's hiding place.

"Mangoes, only forty a kilo. Forty a kilo! Mangoes!" He was definitely in a market. And he definitely knew that accent. Now he was certain. He was in Crask.

Crask. Where Joe had been imprisoned. Crask. Where Trey had been tortured. Crask of Notalia, the land that had invaded Anasius in 316 and sought to destroy her. In the space of two minutes, Jason had gone from starting to message his girlfriend, to hiding under a market stall in the heart of enemy country. He could hardly take in the horror of it.

He took a breath and took stock. Moving from his hiding place would be dangerous. He was not wearing Notalian clothing. He wasn't even wearing Anasiun attire. He would be as obvious as a flamingo in a desert. And if Notalia was anything like it used to be, it would not be long before he was arrested and awaiting the same treatment as Trey in those notorious dungeons. Whatever the reason for his extraction, and however uncomfortable it might get, he needed to stay where he crouched. He was alone, scared, confused and in danger of serious leg cramp.

The conversations around him ebbed and flowed. But it wasn't long before he heard more mentions of Crask. He tried to tune in.

"...Crask. It was very unlucky to lose our top Royals and the Head of our military all in the same month, but Turonia have been so helpful in supporting our leadership, filling in the gaps and helping us put a good government together."

"I don't know about that. Seems to me that the worse they get at decision-making, the wealthier they become."

"Maybe you're right. They are paid well. And Turonia's agreement to invest in Notalia has proved very popular, hasn't it? Think of how far the nation has come just in the last year. Think of how much infrastructure has improved."

"I know," the woman interrupted, sounding exasperated, but also lowering her voice, making it a bit harder for Jason to hear. He shuffled slowly across the cobblestones under the table, making sure he stayed hidden. The woman continued.

"But what if we've handed over control to a foreign nation? Just think, if Turonia pulled out, our government would collapse. And the investment isn't just in trams and stadiums and communications, is it? Your cousin is involved, building subs and armoured vehicles as if there's no tomorrow, and war is just around the corner. I don't like it."

"But a country has to defend itself..."

"Shh, too loud," the woman warned him. "This kind of talk is dangerous." She lowered her voice further. "Who does Notalia need to defend itself from exactly? We have far better military capability than any nation around us except for Turonia itself. Anasius is weak and won't try anything. Juntaou is hemmed in by the mountains. Others would need to cross the sea, and I don't see that happening anytime soon."

"So why are they building all this stuff then, if there's no threat?" the man asked, confused.

"Exactly," the woman responded in a triumphant whisper. "The only possible reason is that we're being annexed by Turonia and they want a firm foothold in the Western continent as a base to conquer others. Turonia is taking over."

"No, no. You've got it all wrong," the man protested, forgetting to keep his voice down. "Turonia have supported us through a difficult phase. They're helping us run the country. They've invested huge amounts. And now we're more advanced and progressive than we've been for a century or more."

"I know," the woman agreed, her voice also raised. "But why? Why have they helped us? Why have they invested so much? It has to be because they're taking over. And anyone who complains is either removed or paid off."

"Hey!" the harsh voice cut across the conversation. "What're you talking about?"

The woman responded smoothly, "Oh, we're just saying how much we've appreciated all the investment here. It's so easy to travel to the market now that the Crask to Downside link is running, and I'm really looking forward to the new stadium opening next month."

"Removed? Paid off?"

"Oh, we were wondering about our mortgage. We were worried we would be removed from our house, but after a generous gift from a friend, it might actually get paid off..."

There was a pause, and Jason couldn't tell if the woman had been convincing enough. "Well," the voice sounded a few seconds later. "Keep your ears to the ground for any treason talk. Turonia would be grateful to you."

"Yes, thank you officer. We will."

And with that, the conversation died and, Jason assumed, the couple departed, leaving the police officer to continue his beat.

As Jason considered what to do next, a little golden circle appeared in the air beside him. It grew rapidly, engulfing Jason, and he found himself back at his desk, his phoned having dropped to the carpet. He bent to retrieve it, mind reeling with all that had happened, but now more determined than ever to talk to Kia. But as he started typing, he was extracted for the second time.

15

Extraction

Kia was agonising for the millionth time over how to respond to Jason. She still loved him, she thought, but she simply did not understand his change of tone the day before. He was meant to support her, for goodness' sake, not add to the distress she was feeling. She started typing a message, but only got to the fourth word.

Elsewhere, Marcia was trying to complete her physics homework. Trey and Max were both flicking idly through social media. Joe and Zika were playing video games at Joe's house. But each experienced that now familiar jerk of electricity and sense of being irresistibly summoned. In a nanosecond, their surroundings disappeared, and they found themselves somewhere in Anasius once more.

When they had recovered from the surprise of all being together, Jason included, it was Max who first realised where they were.

"Hey," he exclaimed. "We're in Arelard Castle again. I think we're in one of those rooms down the corridor from XSHC."

A horde of memories came flooding back to them as he spoke. But they had no time to reminisce, because the doorway opened and a tall but slightly rotund figure came inside, wearing a traditional Anasiun robe and wiping sweat from his brow. He saw the friends gathered by the window.

"Who are you?" he asked, startled. "How did you get here?" His deep voice was strong but tinged with what sounded to the friends like worry.

Joe looked at the others. It was always so hard to explain.

"We've been extracted," he said, accidentally using the friends' term for what happened whenever their phones pulled them into Anasius. "I mean, someone here, royalty probably, has called for us to be here—"

"—Of course," the man at the doorway interrupted him. And then, almost to himself, he remarked, "But I never expected it to happen quite so quickly." He shook his head.

Suddenly, the man didn't seem startled anymore, or worried, or annoyed by the sudden appearance of seven strangers in his private quarters. Instead, he looked like he was working something out, like figuring out a complex maths problem without a calculator. He looked them all up and down, raising his eyebrows as he took in their jeans, tracksuit bottoms and trainers. His eyes nearly popped out of his head when he saw Joe's loud graphic T-shirt. At the same time, the friends considered the man in front of them. He had brown ankle boots with gold laces and a gold ring encircling his right ear. Under the long dark robe, they saw someone under forty with vaguely familiar features...

Trey attempted to take charge.

"Sir," he began, in his American accent. "We know we're only extracted when Anasius is in dire need. What year is it? Who called us here? And who are you?"

Infuriatingly, the man answered Trey with a demand of his own. "Tell me who *you* all are." His voice carried such strength and gravity that it was impossible to refuse. Trey made the introductions. Then, nodding, the man finally said, "The year is 562 and I'm Xci1, Prince of Anasius in the service of Xcion the Sovereign who knows all things."

Xci1 found the reactions around the room virtually impossible to read. One boy was shaking his head in wonder, muttering, "I thought he looked familiar." The girls seemed unable to speak. Another boy, eyes full of emotion, exclaimed, "Amazing – 562? If you think about it, that means we've been alive more than 250 years!"

"Xci1, we are honoured to meet you," Trey said, bowing in deference to the Prince, as did the others as soon as they remembered their manners. "Your words are hard for us to hear, Your Majesty. The last time we were in Anasius was almost 200 years ago, it was 386, and we were helping Prince Arlon to reclaim the throne when he was but sixteen years old. Before that, we came in 318 and helped to repel the Notalian Invasion. If it is 562, all our friends from back then have long since died, and Anasius must have been through all kinds of things – things we know nothing about."

If any common Anasiun citizen hadn't been surprised before his speech, he would be totally floored after it. The idea that the same set of young people had visited across 250 years of Anasiun history would have been too incredible to believe. But Xci1 was no common citizen. He was Xci1, Prince of Anasius, Overlord to the Handed Isles and second only to Xcion the Sovereign. He knew his history very well, not least because it was his personal history.

"King Arlon was my great-grandfather," he told them. This explained why he looked familiar – he had the same high cheekbones and square jaw that Arlon had all those years ago (or last year, depending on how you thought of it). "And I have called you here because, once again, we have a problem. There is an unknown assassin working in Anasius."

The friends looked at each other. An assassin? They braced themselves for what was to come.

"First, he killed our Elder for Security," Xci1 continued. "Then, two weeks later, our Elder for Defence and also Lord Downing, our top army General. Then he killed the Head of XSHC. And then, just this morning, he killed the Elder for Transport. He is targeting senior leaders in Anasius, and we are confident he is not going to stop his killing spree until we catch him.

"Come," he ordered, without taking a breath. "Let me introduce you to the team." And without any more explanation, he strode from the room, assuming these youngsters would follow obediently as would any of his subjects.

And follow him they did, out of the room, along the corridor, through some double doors which had never been there before, and up to the door of XSHC. It was a much larger door with a much larger security lock than the friends remembered – keypad, retinal scan, and a security officer standing directly outside, armed with an electric baton and what looked like it might be a taser of some kind.

At the sight of Xci1, the security officer stepped aside, typed on the keypad and waited for Xci1 to offer his eye to the scanner. The lock clicked and, less than five minutes from their sudden arrival, all seven friends were ushered into XSHC.

*

Half an hour later, after the security personnel's shock had passed, the friends were all wearing the traditional Anasiun robe, long black boots and buttonless shirt and breeches. They were now each deep in conversation with different people. Kia was talking to Chines, the interim Head of XSHC, asking for an update on how it had changed since she oversaw the overthrow of Mary Stroud and the coronation of King Arlon. The conversation was so distracting that Chines almost forgot the resignation letter that was burning a hole in the breast pocket of his robe. As they spoke, Kia touched the golden ring wrapped around her right ear. Each of the friends had also been taken to the implant room and given their implants – the communication device all Anasiuns received at birth, allowing them to communicate freely. Having the rings on their ears once again felt comforting, like putting on summer clothes after the winter.

Joe and Jason were with Xci1, who had pulled them aside to discuss an idea with them. But despite conversing with royalty, Jason felt his eyes drifting over the man's shoulder to the back of Kia's dark brown head. He was frustrated to be so near to her and yet be unable to discuss things that seemed much more important. She seemed to be giving him the cold shoulder, and he understood why. If they could just have a proper conversation, then she would understand.

Trey, Max, Marcia and Zika meanwhile had discovered something important. The Commissioner had pulled up the roster of significant state and royal occasions for the coming two months, and they spent some time trying to work out who was the next most likely target for assassination. Whilst there were three or four possibilities, eventually all of them were convinced of who it was. If the aim was to overthrow the leadership of Anasius, then one candidate stood out above the rest as the most obvious primary target. And they knew the likely location, the date and the time. But for the life of them, they couldn't figure out how to prevent it without alerting the assassin that they were onto him. They knew they needed an urgent discussion with Xci1, but he was in deep conversation with Jason and Joe.

In the meantime, they collated physical maps, for detailed plans of the day, and all the information from previous events they could get their hands on. Soon, scattered around the large central table, maps were spread out, papers were littered and much head-scratching was being undertaken. It would require every brain cell they had between them if they were to succeed.

Xci1 rose to his feet, straightened his robe and called them to order.

"Ladies and Gentlemen," he began, but stopped again as he saw Chines approaching him. He checked his irritation – he was not familiar with being interrupted.

"Chines?"

Chines coughed.

"Your Highness, despite all my best efforts and crazy hours of the last few weeks, the Elder for Transport was killed on my watch. I did everything I could, and it was not enough. I am not the person for this job, so I am tendering my resignation with immediate effect. I will, of course, serve Anasius to the best of my ability, whether still within XSHC or outside of it." Chines offered him the letter.

There was silence in the room. Three Elders killed. Lord Downing killed. Patricia killed. And now Chines stepping down. What would XSHC do now?

Xci1 looked Chines in the eye but did not extend his hand to receive the envelope.

"Of course, you are free to do so," he said carefully. "But I do not accept your letter."

Chines put it back in his cloak pocket, feeling embarrassed and confused in equal measure. How could Xci1 refuse? But Xci1 didn't give him time to ask.

"Let me observe," Xci1 began. "The Elder for Transport did not die because of any incompetence, Chines, but because of his own refusal to listen to your sage advice. His death is not your responsibility. The previous deaths, too, are the result of some careful planning from a ruthless assassin who will stop at nothing to achieve his ends, whatever those ends may be. Their deaths are not on you either. We have thought long and hard and had no success, which is why I made the royal call for help. So, Chines, this difficult series of events is not about you."

Xci1 took a moment to let this sink in.

"I spent some time last night studying Anasiun history – some very specific history, in fact. I discovered that the previous royal calls for help were made in 316 and in 386, and on both occasions, Xcion the Sovereign gave us these young people from a different world." A murmur spread across the room, but he raised his hand for quiet.

"I know, I know, it is hard to comprehend. But the more I studied, the more obvious it became. These seven teenagers who have joined us here are the same group who came before. Indeed, in 316 there was an eighth, but tragically, he died halfway through their fight against the Notalians."

The friends tensed as Xci1 spoke of Zak in all but name. For them, just being in Anasius always brought back memories of Zak.

"Everyone," Xci1 continued, "Xcion the Sovereign has sent us these young people because we need their perspective, their fresh eyes and their lack of assumptions. I know now that they have experiences none of us can match. Chines has worked here in the shelter of Arelard Castle ever since his graduation. These young people are not even old enough to be in the academy, and yet some of them graduated from the Overlord Academy back in 316. Of those graduates, one became an officer for the academy, two went on active duty, and one was then further trained in the highly secretive and highly specialist Underlord Academy, which went out of existence back in 370 and has since been replaced. Their work through 316 is the prime reason Anasius survived the Notalian Invasion, especially Jason's work in repelling the Notalian advance at Ruwark, and the efforts of Joe, Trey, Marcia, Kia, Max and Zika as Tsarn made its last stand. In 381, they executed carefully laid plans to infiltrate this very castle, they broke into the royal vaults, and they brought down the empire of one Mary Stroud, who was seeking to become the overall ruler not just of Anasius, but of Parlemoni and Notalia as well. They achieved that by exposing her for who she was – a power-hungry fraudster who had orchestrated the murder of the entire royal family at the Summer Palace. It was only because of their work that Arlon survived those six years and then became king. We owe them a great national debt, even if they achieve nothing this time around."

The friends looked at the floor and shuffled their feet. Trey found himself breaking into Xci1's monologue.

"Your Highness, our efforts in 386 were almost entirely useless, to be honest. Our break-in to the royal vault failed. We only made it into this castle by dumb luck, and the great achievement you lay at our feet really came about through Arlon's determination and Melek's martyrdom."

Xci1 looked at him with a strange expression, tilting his head.

"I thought you didn't believe in dumb luck?" he asked, his eye twinkling.

"Well..."

"The fact is," Xci1 continued, "Xcion the Sovereign brought everything together as he always does and saved us from disaster. But that salvation came about in large part due to your work and willingness, whether or not you accept the accolade."

He addressed the whole room again. "Ladies and Gentlemen, whatever else you may think, know these young people are highly experienced. They know what it is to fight a war. They know what it is to lose comrades, both on and off the battlefield. They understand what is at stake for the good of the country. And they are willing to fight for it, come what may. That is why they are here. Their role is to help us, inspire us and, ultimately, lead us to success."

He turned back to Chines. "Chines, I am not going to accept your resignation until we have overturned Turonia's plans. But I am going to allow you to return to your former role as Deputy Head of XSHC in this interim period. Now tell me, what were you discussing with Kia?"

Chines was confused, unsure how his recent conversation with a teenage girl had any bearing on what they needed to do next.

"Well, Your Highness...she was asking me what has changed here at XSHC in the past 150 years. I was explaining our recent technology upgrade."

Xci1 was looking at Kia, who met his eye.

"Kia, you worked here at XSHC back in 316 and again in 386?"

"Yes, sir."

"As we work towards finding this assassin and dealing with him, would you be prepared to step up and lead XSHC for the next little while?"

Kia stared at him as if he had gone mad.

"But, but I..." She cleared her throat, tried again. "Your Highness, what on earth makes you think I can do that in my condition?"

Xci1 raised his eyebrows.

"In your condition?"

"Well, I mean...I'm not even seventeen," she said lamely, trying to backpedal, firmly avoiding Jason's gaze. Xci1's brow furrowed.

"Kia, you have done it twice before, and you were younger then. You oversaw the war in 316. You planned and oversaw most of the overthrow of Stroud in 386. You're the only one here with both the skills *and* the experience to go with it. I could not be putting XSHC in more capable hands."

Kia went red for the second time. There was an awkward silence.

"Of course, Your Highness. I will serve as best I can," she said.

"Good," Xci1 returned, clapping his hands together. "Now, I need to speak with Jason and Joe. Everyone else: we must locate and eliminate this assassin as soon as possible. There is a great deal to be done."

16

Xci1's Little Idea

Jason looked at Joe as they joined Xci1 at a corner desk. Why had they been selected?

"Gentlemen, I must fill you in on our enemy," Xci1 began. "For some time, I have suspected that Turonia is trying to take over the southern continent. I have watched the slow but steady decline in leadership in Notalia over the last two years. First, the General's death, then the Minister's surprise retirement...And then the rapid promotion of newcomers to their cabinet. Plus, Notalia's huge growth in transport and communication seems significantly beyond their means. I have always wondered whether the Emperor of Turonia has had something to do with it, and now I fear the same thing may be happening to Anasius..."

As Xci1 spoke, Jason's nods grew increasingly more violent. He knew better than to interrupt a Xci, but the information in his head was bursting to come out. Xci1 looked at the eager young teenager.

"You're exactly right," Jason blurted, forgetting to use the royal title. "And I know it."

Joe looked at him with raised eyebrows. How could Jason possibly know anything about it?

"The thing is," Jason explained. "I was extracted earlier today. To Crask—"

"—What?"

Joe felt a flood of cold over his body. "Crask?"

But Jason had held up his hand and continued to explain what he had heard from beneath the stall at the marketplace. Xci1 gave a low whistle.

"That confirms it," he said. "It's a slow takeover and a clever one. Pay people large amounts to implement your policies. Invest to keep the general populace happy. Slowly gain control of the government and therefore the country. No-one complains because no-one has any reason to."

Joe shivered. It reminded him of the biology class where his teacher, Mr Shaw, had explained that you don't kill a frog by throwing it in boiling water – it will just jump out. But place it in room temperature water and heat it to boiling point and the frog won't notice. It will slowly cook to death. This new threat to Anasius was less obvious than the previous two, but no less deadly. The water was heating up.

"And hence the assassin," Jason added.

"What do you mean?" Joe wasn't sure how an assassin fitted into this covert war.

Xci1's usually ruddy face was grey. "It seems that it's no longer just about paying people who promote Turonian ideals and push for greater diplomatic ties with them. It's worse than that. Turonia is getting impatient. People either accept payment for promoting what Turonia want, or they're...removed. That's why Notalia's General died. That's why the Deputy Prime Minister resigned and gave way to someone far younger. And that's why we have an assassin who has already killed three Elders, a senior military official and our Head of this XSHC. How can they take control if the people in power are resistant to their suggestions?"

"But why did you want to talk to Joe and me about this?" Jason became aware that the rest of the group, including Kia, were still behind them, talking to the security elders about the assassin's next target.

Xci1 smiled slightly.

"I had a little idea." He leant closer, lowering his voice. "We have to use every weapon we have in this fight and you two are our next weapon."

There was silence for a few moments whilst Xci1 collected his thoughts. Joe felt a rush of adrenaline. He sensed an adventure ahead.

"We need to find a way for you both to infiltrate Turonia and try to discover the assassin's identity from their end."

Jason's mouth fell open. Joe's heart picked up pace.

"But the assassin is *here*," Jason protested. "On foreign soil we'd be trying to find someone who isn't there. Besides, Turonia is huge."

"We don't need to just catch this assassin, we need to know more about why they have been sent in the first place, we need to get into the heart of Turonia's intentions," Xci1 responded. "And I have information that will narrow the field in Turonia. Three months ago, I met the Turonian Emperor. I was a guest at the Tournament for the Order of the

Dragon. It's a remarkable, relentless and brutal tournament. Their very best fighters compete for the title of champion. Each competitor is under training from the Order of the Dragon – a secret society based in the south of the country. At the OOD, the monks train their students in every form of combat imaginable. And I know that if Turonia is using assassins to take out foreign leaders, those assassins will come from the Order of the Dragon."

Jason began to understand.

"Hang on a moment," he asked. "Are you seriously asking us, a couple of untrained high-school kids, to try and infiltrate a school of expertly trained fighters? We'd be mincemeat."

Xci1 almost laughed. "But you're not untrained. You've both been through the Overlord Academy. It's why I chose you."

"We can handle ourselves," Joe said.

"That's alright for you to say," Jason returned. "You're still involved in sport at school, and you train a few times every week. I don't. I just sit around and eat rubbish. I'm not battle-ready, not by any stretch."

Xci1 just grinned. "I suspect you remember more of your training than you think, Jason. And anyway, you're here to help, after all."

Jason and Joe looked at each other. What in the world were they getting themselves into?

17

Making Plans

As Trey, Max, Marcia and Zika continued to study the maps, they remained certain they knew who the next target was. They looked at Xci1 talking to Jason and Joe. They looked at each other. How to interrupt a Royal? Trey coughed.

"Yes?" Xci1 looked across the room.

"Your Majesty," Max responded, much to everyone's surprise. Max usually only spoke when directly spoken to. "We've examined all the scheduled civic and royal visits in the coming two months. And it seems that by far the most obvious event and therefore the most obvious target is..."

"It's you, Your Majesty." Trey took over. "At the Winter Pageant in Ruwark."

Xci1 put his hands onto the chair in front of him and leant on it whilst he thought, his brow wrinkled. There was a silence.

"Well," he began slowly, "I should have guessed." Another pause. "And the event hasn't changed much in the last decade since the death of my grandfather, Xcion preserve him, so the assassin's got plenty to work with. He'll already know the usual carnival routes, the exact location of the podium, the usual placing of security." He stopped and then looked across expectantly at the Police Commissioner. "Do you have a plan?"

But it was Kia who spoke out, as was often the case when she felt responsible. "What if you didn't give the speech? The event could be opened by a local dignitary – maybe the Mayor of Ruwark – and it would be easy to keep you safe that way." Even as she spoke, she knew from Xci1's face that it was useless.

Xci1 shook his head. "No," his voice was firm. "I will not be cowed by the threat of an attack. The pageant has been opened by a Xci for nearly thirty years, and I'm not about to change that tradition simply because I'm worried about my own skin. And I will not put anyone else's life on the line. Anyway, we are working hard to avoid sending our people into panic, remember? What possible excuse could we give for me to avoid it? I'm perfectly healthy, my speech is already written and I am going to give it."

Trey raised his eyebrows at the others. They had thought this would happen. The Commissioner's forehead was etched with worry. Surely keeping Xci1 safe was more important than the usual protocol for a pageant? He wiped the sweat from his brow. This day was not panning out at all in the way he had imagined.

*

A few hours later, they had finalised a plan to catch the assassin. And, despite arguing about it, Xci1 wouldn't be giving the speech after all. He had vehemently fought the idea that someone would act as a stand-in for him, but Trey had taken him aside and, after an in-depth conversation, Xci1 had eventually seemed to accept that it was in Anasius' best interests to keep him safe. So, instead, with his trademark diplomacy, Xci1 had secured the use of specialist Juntaou body armour and a mask which could replicate his body and face with extreme accuracy. Wearing the armour and mask, a stand-in would give his speech at the Winter Pageant whilst security personnel would hunt for the assassin. It was risky, delicate, and someone could definitely die. But it was the only idea they had.

Before leaving for Dhanges, the capital city of Juntaou, to begin work on the mask, Xci1 called Xcion Strategic High Command to order one last time.

"Friends, our plan is a fragile one. At any point the assassin could slip through our fingers. And we need to know more about why he was sent in the first place." He looked at Joe and Jason. "This is why I propose a second plan."

He explained about the Order of the Dragon, and his idea of sending two spies to infiltrate their training grounds and gather intel about a Turonian takeover of the southern continent.

"But who would ever agree to do something so dangerous?" Marcia asked with wide eyes after he had finished.

Jason and Joe looked at each other. Joe looked at Xci1. Jason didn't look at Kia.

"We would," Jason said.

Kia gasped. "No. You have no chance against a hundred highly trained soldiers. It's suicide."

"We're the only ones with the experience, Kia," Joe said.

But Kia shook her head. The idea of Jason heading off on a dangerous mission was not only terrifying, but she suddenly knew, without a shadow of a doubt, that she loved him just as much as she ever had. Who knew what might happen to him?

"Kia's not completely wrong though." Xci1 looked at Jason and Joe, appraising their youth with a frown. "It's a risky endeavour, terribly risky. Turonia are a fierce nation. They have never attempted diplomatic discussions with us, they are not signed up to the southern continent treaties, and they seem prejudiced against our ways of life – not to mention that they are governed by a ruthless Emperor. He rules with an iron fist, and the Herculean Order – his police force – ensure that citizens live according to the law, and in fear of them. The HO are paid handsomely for their work, as are his most trusted advisors who vie for his favour.

"When the Emperor dies," he continued, "his authority will pass to his eldest son who is even more ruthless than his father. The general running of the country is given to ten Ministers, all of them selected by the Emperor or by his father before him. Ministers never marry and they rule for life, wielding a huge amount of influence over Turonia. For all of them, security is very tight. The Emperor, his wives, children and the ten Ministers live at Womak Castle in the north of Turonia - a huge forbidding building that covers nearly an acre of land. It is a modern-day fortress and utterly impregnable. The Ministers never leave it. The Emperor leaves only for official visits, and there are only three of those in any given year. The security personnel at the castle are highly trained, and patrol the building twenty-four hours a day, seven days a week. Food is supplied daily by truck, arrives at the external security complex, and is examined, tested and resealed before it is allowed within the castle walls. Most visitors do not enter the castle. They arrive at the security complex and speak with the Ministers or even the Emperor himself by holographic video link."

The friends were stunned into silence. They had never heard of such brutal, controlled rule.

"The Order of the Dragon is even worse. They take children from a young age to use them for some nefarious purpose. They spend a huge amount of time training them. And this is not just self-defence. This is careful training designed to prepare them for hand-to-hand combat. I think that they train somewhere in the south of the country - somewhere fairly remote. If we can locate them, we can gather information to help us identify our assassin and understand Turonia's intentions. Their training ground won't be nearly as securely guarded as Womak Castle. We may have a chance of success."

Kia was feeling sick again, although she was unsure this time whether it was to do with her condition, or to do with the boys thinking about infiltrating an enemy country where they'd be surrounded by top-flight fighters. She asked for some water.

"Of course," Xci1 responded, pointing across to a shelf in the corner which held numerous refreshments. He gestured and a couple of older men on a nearby desk rose to attend to the young people, much to Kia's relief.

"Your Highness," she said, sipping her water. "What if we can locate the Order of the Dragon from live satellite imagery? Maybe we wouldn't need to send anyone at all. If not, perhaps we could send maybe two of your advanced police force?" She couldn't entertain the thought of Jason and Joe going to Turonia.

But Xci1 didn't bite. "It won't be enough. I know you have to continue planning for the Winter Pageant, Kia, but in your role as interim Head of XSHC you'll need to oversee this possible incursion into Turonia as well. Can you do that?" he asked.

But Kia was unable to respond. She was being asked to run a mission at Ruwark to try and capture a trained assassin, putting her own friends in significant danger. Now she was being asked to plan an incursion into a compound where dozens of fighters were trained every day. She was being asked to put her own boyfriend into that situation. And on top of all that she was struggling with her own circumstances. Suddenly, sickness rose in her. She stood up, her chair falling to the ground. Mumbling an apology, she rushed from the room. The others looked at each other.

"Your Highness, Kia isn't fully well," Jason jumped in. "Head of XSHC is a massive ask, but I know she can do it. She will do it. As her friends, we know she is capable of the task. I'll go and chat to her."

"No," Marcia said. "*I'll* go and chat to her. She'll be in the girls' toilets."

Jason frowned but Marcia was already leaving.

Marcia could hear Kia being sick in the bathroom. Kia didn't know if it was because of her condition or because of what might happen to Jason or because of what she was being asked to do. But the three things together made her head swim.

Marcia opened the bathroom door. "Kia, are you okay?"

Kia almost laughed. She wiped her mouth with some tissue.

"Not exactly," she said. She flushed the toilet and opened the stall door, coming out to her reflection in the huge mirror over the sinks. "Ugh," she said as she caught sight of her face. "I'm a mess."

Marcia grinned. "I can't think of a single person who would agree with that," she said, making Kia smile in spite of herself.

"We were extracted so that we could help in whatever way we can," Kia said, washing her hands. "But what Xci1 is asking seems impossible."

"It always seems impossible," Marcia countered. Kia put her hands on the sink and thought for a minute.

"Yes," she said. "I've had to step up before even though I was scared and didn't know what was going to happen.

Somehow, everything worked out." As she spoke, her courage and determination seemed to build. "The worst thing about this plan is that it'll put Jason and Joe in danger. But that's happened before too and Xcion has always kept them safe. I think I need to just dig deep and try and do this thing."

Marcia breathed her admiration. How Kia could have such strength was beyond her.

"You won't be alone," Marcia said. "I'll do anything I can to help. I know I don't have your brains, but I'll support in every way I can."

"Thanks, Marcia," Kia responded. "Although, given your last set of exam results, I think you're underselling your intelligence..." She swept her hair from her face and smiled at her friend.

Back at the XSHC office, there was silence as they waited. "Perhaps I've put too much on Kia's shoulders," Xci1 said after a few minutes, suddenly looking tired. "If my reading of history is correct, she oversaw operations in Ruwark, Port Diblaine and Tsarn virtually simultaneously back in 316. But she seems less certain than the history books record – less self-assured and more...I don't know...more..." but he was interrupted again. Marcia re-entered the room, closely followed by Kia. She was pale, slightly green, but her eyes were determined.

"I'm sorry for the interruption, Your Highness," she said. "I will oversee the Winter Pageant and the incursion into Turonia. I apologise, I have not been feeling quite myself recently." She glanced over at Jason as she spoke.

"What an understatement," Jason thought.

Kia crossed to the nearest computer desk and sat down, pulling the keyboard out. If Jason was going to do this, she was going to give him all the help she could.

"Let's find this Order of the Dragon training ground."

A large map of the northern shore of Anasius appeared on the screen, with the edge of Ruwark towards the top of the screen, the wide beach on the shoreline, and then the ocean extending to the bottom of the screen. But this was no ordinary map. This was real-life video in great detail from a satellite a few miles up. Using two fingers and the touchscreen on the computer, you could zoom out to see the whole southern continent and northern territories, including Turonia. As you zoomed in, you began to see trams and buses and people and waves of the sea and boats on the river and flags flying and trees moving in the breeze – all happening in real time. It was incredible.

Kia zoomed out until the southern coast and a good bit of the country of Turonia came into view again, just thirty miles across the sea. Xci1 directed her.

"The tournament happens at Narkon, a city to the north. The Emperor mentioned that the Womak Castle complex is a couple of miles outside Narkon. And when I was at the tournament, I got the impression that the training ground for the Order of the Dragon was not too far from there, since the combatants went home in the evening and returned the following day. It could lie further south, but it may be quite well camouflaged..."

Distracting herself from her nausea and inner conflict, Kia focused all her attention on the mission in hand. She rapidly zoomed in and out on various locations, but, after a few minutes of this, found nothing.

An older man with a greying beard spoke up from the edge of the room, "Perhaps the whole training camp is underground?"

Silence followed.

"Looking at the bronzed skin of those fighters at the tournament, and knowing how pasty-white most Turonians are, I am convinced the majority of their training was conducted outside," Xci1 responded. "We need more eyes on this."

He divvied out sections of the map to different groups of the XSHC security, and they jumped onto individual computers, zooming into things that looked promising and then zooming out again to find something else. One or two places were projected onto the big screen, but on further examination both were rejected. It was a full half-hour of studying before the group working on sector four pushed onto the big screen something which looked more promising. As soon as they did, everyone in the room stopped working. Kia took control of the screen.

The screen showed a large group of people, evenly spaced in a clearing in the woods. With a vertical view, it was impossible to see full faces, but something of what they were wearing, the colour of their hair and how they moved was distinguishable. In fact, the presence of the large group of people was the only reason the area had been noticed at all. Again, the teenagers were astounded by the resolution they could see from a real-time satellite camera.

Kia zoomed out a little from the group on the ground, and at first all she could see were trees, with the occasional black rectangle here and there. But then she realised that there were three long buildings on opposite sides of a courtyard, with a couple of others more haphazardly placed inside it, each carefully disguised to make it look like the aerial view of the trees around them. The black rectangles were skylights, providing light to the rooms in the buildings below them. You could just pick out the edges and corners of the buildings. One side of the compound was a vertical wall, perhaps half-a-metre wide, with a wider part in the middle. Again, it was carefully painted to blend in with the surroundings. But there was a track leading from the compound to a highway that connected a river port to the capital city. Womak Castle was only half a mile away, although the majority of the land in between was thick brush with no tracks or trails – clearly there was no road from Womak to the Order of the Dragon. The eastern side of the compound sat near the edge of a wide river, which came right up to the eastern wall at one point. So it appeared that there could be access via the river, as well as by road.

Everyone at XSHC was convinced. This was the location of the Order of the Dragon.

18

The Winter Pageant

Zika was halfway up the scaffolding at the Ruwark Needle building site. His stomach swirled as he glanced down. He was up the road from the city hospital and across the park from the Summer Palace. When completed, the Needle was going to be 200 metres high, with a high-speed elevator taking ten passengers only twenty seconds to reach the top. The viewing gallery just below its peak would provide a panoramic view over the Summer Palace and beyond to the northern sea. On a clear day, it was expected that the southern shores of Turonia would be visible, thirty miles away. Ruwark's Needle was due to be opened in 563, replacing a smaller monument erected to commemorate the massacre of the Royals at the Summer Palace in 381. It was also intended to commemorate the lives lost in other conflicts since, especially the battle to protect the Handed Isles which finished just fourteen years earlier. The tower had almost reached its full height, and the scaffolding around it drove majestically into the sky.

Zika had been in place for hours, balancing on the wooden beams. He was scanning the scene and training his binoculars on anything and everything, trying to anticipate where the assassin would position himself. The XSHC had conducted an extensive survey of the area under Kia's watchful eye, and, confident a long-range rifle would be used following Patricia van Olden's death, she had insisted they focus on any high structures within a half-mile radius. The Needle scaffold was the most obvious place, but with security in place around the perimeter and Zika halfway up a good four hours before the event, they were confident the assassin would find a different vantage point.

*

A day earlier, Max, known for his diplomacy and listening skills, had sat in front of a tall man with unusually bushy eyebrows. There was a confidentiality document on the desk between them, untouched.

"Let me get this straight," the man began, swallowing. "You want me to stand at the podium, impersonate Xci1, deliver his speech and hope that I get shot so that you have a chance of catching the marksman?"

Max suppressed a smile. "The scientists tell us that although a bullet would be painful, the graphene mask and the body armour should keep you safe."

"*Should?*"

"Look," Max leant forward. "It's our job to protect Xci1's life at all costs. It took the royal family over 100 years to recover fully from the massacre of 381, and their lives are of more importance in the governance of Anasius than the lives of anyone else, you and I included."

There was a silence as the actor absorbed all that he'd been told in the last hour. Assassins. Juntaou body armour. Masks. *Rifles*. Rifles in Anasius. This was not his usual acting gig. He understood now why they had offered him so much money.

Max decided to change tack.

"We can look for someone else, but you were specially recommended to us not just because of your skill, but because of your loyalty. We're trying to protect Xci1, catch the assassin who is targeting our leadership, and put Anasius on an even footing for the future. We're not asking you to do this for money, we're asking you to do this for your country."

Max wondered to himself what would happen if the shooter used armour-piercing rounds – surely the graphene would be no use then? But he didn't mention it.

"I'm no soldier, but I'm also no coward," the man said, fingering a hole in his shirt, bushy eyebrows furrowed. He thought of his wife. His children. How proud they would be.

"Are you sure I will be safe?"

"Your body armour is the highest quality in existence," Max replied. Then added, "The ambulance used in the charade will be a real ambulance."

"What an answer." The man gave a hollow laugh. Then he stood up, turned from Max and faced the window. He doubted the boy in front of him knew it, but he had long been wanting to do something more meaningful with his life, something for Xcion. The feeling had begun to burn in his quiet moments, as he came home from work, picked up a cup of tea, or closed his eyes at night...Perhaps this was Xcion's answer? His wife's eyes swam into his vision once more.

There was a long silence. So long that Max began to wonder whether the man had forgotten he was there. But then, when he turned from the window, his face had softened.

"If my wife and children will be provided for, I'll do it."

Max nodded and pushed the document across the desk towards him. "Already taken care of."

They had less than twenty-four hours to prepare him for the event, and Max insisted on overseeing every part of it.

*

The motorcade stopped at the crossing of Fourth Street and Seventh Street, almost a minute ahead of the official schedule. They took slightly longer than expected to pull away from the junction, and they slowed again to a crawl as they approached the Summer Palace. Nevertheless, when the second car pulled up to the curb, they were almost exactly on time. Security personnel across the area had moved to high alert as the vehicles came into view. And so began the choreography that is any royal visit.

Max knew that a person is often easily recognised by their gait. He realised that whilst the actor and Xci1 looked virtually identical, they walked in very different ways. So when the team of bodyguards opened the door and surrounded "Xci1" to escort him to the podium, the fact that no-one could see how he was walking was part of the plan.

The actor moved across to the podium, took out a pair of reading glasses – the actor's glasses were simply glass, he really had no need of them – and prepared for the best performance of his career.

"Really," thought Zika from his perch up on the scaffolding. "He does look exactly like Xci1. Those make-up artists are amazing." He hoped the voice coaching had been equally effective. He had the new Z4 Anasiun binoculars glued to his eyes, giving him nearly perfect sight as he zoomed in and out, scanning the surrounding buildings, looking for anything unusual, anyone seemingly out of place, anything that looked different from when he had begun his vigil.

Everyone else was in place. Kia was a hundred miles away, standing in XSHC watching the moving images from all the cameras around the Summer Palace and beyond. She was accompanied by nervous senior security advisors. Marcia was in a tram below City Hall, waiting to pick up Max, Zika and, hopefully, Trey and return them to Arelard when their jobs were done. Trey was waiting in the ambulance to the side of the forecourt.

The shouting and cheering and noise and buzz from the crowd died away as Xci1 approached the podium. The next twenty minutes were going to be crucial. His voice came loud and clear over the loudspeaker system. It was deep, sonorous and unmistakably royal. "I didn't need to worry about his voice," thought Zika as he listened in via his implant, touching the gold ring around his ear that was now emitting a soft glow. Every inflection, every pause, every filler word was exactly like Xci1.

"Friends, delegates, citizens, visitors, people of Anasius, I greet you in the name of Xcion the Sovereign. May I offer the warmest of welcomes to this our twenty-eighth Winter Pageant. I am delighted to be able to welcome so many artists, dancers, musicians, acrobats, artisans and craftsmen to what is, I am reliably informed, the greatest and longest carnival Anasius has ever seen. We will look back over the past year and give thanks for all we have endured and enjoyed. And we will look ahead to—"

And then it came.

The voice died away, and with just a faint look of surprise on his face, he fell. The bullet had hit him square on the forehead. Within moments, the bodyguards and on-call doctor enclosed him. He was carried to the waiting ambulance, where Trey waited to meet them.

Zika descended the scaffolding and took the short distance to the Summer Palace at a run. Frustration coursed through him. He had noticed nothing from the scaffolding on Ruwark Needle, despite having had a perfect view of the palace, a perfect view of all the buildings around, and a perfect view of the carnival and all its floats that were snaking their way around the side streets leading up to the palace. He had studied the buildings, especially the upper windows and roofs. He had studied the park and its trees, looking for anyone who might be sitting up a tree in camouflage gear. He had watched the preparations and the lining up of the carnival, taking particular note of the first few floats and acts which had a direct line of sight to the podium when the replacement Xci1 arrived in the motorcade. But he had seen nothing. Now he wanted to look at the footage which he knew was being replayed in the security hub in the Summer Palace. What had he missed?

The ambulance arrived at the hospital three minutes later. Security personnel surrounded his bed as "Xci1" was wheeled through the emergency-wing doors, in the lift and up to the second floor, and then down the corridor and into a secure room for treatment. The charade continued, even as the real Xci1 remained in the tram siding beneath the Summer Palace, awaiting information from Kia back at Arelard Castle.

The doors closed behind "Xci1's" bed, and four security personnel stood outside the door with three more inside, along with two doctors and three nurses, all carefully screened for the job. After exiting the ambulance, Trey waited in the hospital security office, watching the screens like a hawk, especially those from cameras at the hospital's main entrance and the exit doors on the north side. He did not expect to see anyone attempting to enter through the emergency wing – the main entrance would be much more straightforward for the assassin to slip through. Trey was dressed in dark breeches, black shoes and a stiff white-collared top with "Security" emblazoned across the back.

As his gaze shifted from screen to screen, Trey recalled all the security footage he had watched over and over again back at Arelard Castle: the assassinations of the Elder for

Security in Ducal City and of the Elder for Defence in Xanver. In each case, as he surveyed the gathered crowds, he had noticed what looked like the same small figure, not much more than a child, in nondescript clothing with a hooded cape hiding the features. Could it be a coincidence? Whilst the official profiling of the assassin had suggested certain characteristics, Trey had a very different idea in mind, an idea so unlikely that he had been worried about sharing it with anyone else. He would probably just be laughed at.

All security personnel, whether uniformed or in plain clothes, were fitted with individual trackers so that the security office knew where they all were at any time, and the team back at Arelard Castle could follow them as well. As usual, the hospital was busy. Every few minutes, one of the security team raced to intercept an arriving patient. They would question them, search them, and then, if satisfied they posed no threat, allow them to move further into the hospital. One or two were turned away and asked to return later in the day. Almost all those stopped were men in their mid to late twenties who were obviously of Turonian descent, or at least very white-skinned and blonde. Trey, though, was looking for something else.

Suddenly he stiffened. A young teenager had shuffled through the main doors, holding what looked like a bandaged arm and shuffling towards the lifts. He stared at her for a few seconds longer. Something was off about her. On noticing a distinct shape under her cloak, he pointed and mumbled something about "checking her out." He disappeared from the security room.

Trey was an only child, used to doing things alone. And having moved to the UK only a year or two earlier, he was used to having to stand on his own two feet. But despite this, he'd always struggled with needing verification of his ideas before sharing them more widely, and this situation was no different. He shook the doubts out of his head and raced down the corridor and around the corner to the lifts. The door to the second lift was already shut as he arrived, and so he watched as the arrow pinged from the first to the second to the third floor and then stopped. He bounded up the stairs like an Olympic athlete. As he turned the corner on the third floor, he caught a glimpse of her blonde head and realised what it was that had bothered him. She didn't have a ring on either ear. She wasn't Anasiun.

Heart racing hard now, he ran to the double doors and pushed at them. They opened noiselessly and he slipped through. Had he lost her? No, the girl was just disappearing through a door on the left, and the shape he thought he had seen under her shirt was now unmistakeable. A gun. Trey had the presence of mind to press on his tracker button to alert security downstairs. He ran as quickly and silently as he could to the door and hesitated. Did this door have any other exits? He didn't want to trap himself with a known assassin. But he didn't want her to get away from him or find her way to Xci1's room which, he estimated, was almost directly below him. He pressed the button on his tracker repeatedly. Where was the backup?

Before he could move, he heard a noise coming from the room. It was the sound of furniture being dragged across the tiled floor. Then there was a moment of silence, followed by the sound of an electric screwdriver. Then a clatter and a straining noise. What in the world was she doing? Trey looked behind him at the empty corridor. He couldn't wait any longer. He opened the door as silently and swiftly as he could, pushing it closed behind him and dropping the emergency catch so that she could not get out. Most rooms had these catches which engaged in an emergency and could only be opened remotely by those in the security office down on the ground floor. He knew he couldn't get out if he needed to, but neither could the girl.

She whirled around at the sound of the lock clicking and came face to face with Trey. She was even younger than he had imagined, perhaps in her very early teens. Her small features were pinched into a scowl. The bandage on her arm was discarded and she was kneeling beside a hole she had opened in the floor – some sort of maintenance hatch. It was clear that she had been pushing wires into a grey block positioned beneath the hatch. Now she began to reach up inside her cloak for something.

"I wouldn't do that if I were you," Trey warned her with a sudden flash of inspiration, his hand already beneath his cloak and pushing outwards on the material. His heart was pounding. "You're not the only one who is armed." He saw the hesitation on her face, and at the same time he realised the genius of her plan.

They were directly above the room where Xci1 lay. The hatch would lead her right to him.

*

"He can't have a firearm," Hera thought, staring at the boy in front of her, her mind racing. But she couldn't be sure. The boy's accent was certainly strange to her ears - what if he didn't belong to a country in the All-nations Arms Agreement? She ran her eyes over him and, despite his height, she decided to ignore him. She could take him if it came to it. Her mission was to make sure Xci1 was dead. Those were her orders.

As they stared at each other, she flicked the switch by her foot and blew a hole in the floor.

*

Debris rained down on Xci1's bed. The security detail sprang to their feet in shock, but before they could act, a figure dropped through the hole, pulled a weapon from their cloak and fired a shot into Xci1's prone body - all before they had hit the ground. The figure rolled and started to get up.

Trey's response was immediate. He sprang and dropped through the hole milliseconds after she did, landing awkwardly. Before she could take a second shot, this strange boy from upstairs had rolled into her legs with a crash and sent her back to the ground, her weapon pinging from her hand and spinning across the floor. His blood was pumping. He would do whatever it took to protect Xci1. The security guards were stunned at the speed of events, hardly having time to react as the girl twisted with rage. Trey grappled with her and tried to pin her arms to her sides, but she had a whole arsenal of martial-arts training moves at her disposal. Despite his considerable weight advantage, Trey had no hope of holding her down.

By now, though, the two security officers had recovered themselves and moved in. And despite her strength and agility, the concerted effort of two grown men twice her weight, coupled with a six-foot and fearless teenager, resulted in her being caught and tied up in minutes. When he thought about it later, Trey reckoned her heart was not really in the fight anyway. Her face betrayed her total confusion. She had realised that Xci1 was not in the bed, but rather standing off to one side, smiling slightly and gazing at her with interest.

As soon as "Xci1" had entered the hospital room a few minutes previous, he'd closed the blinds on the windows and made up the bed with rolled blankets and a pre-prepared wig and mask to look like he was lying down, still unconscious. He'd pushed the bed to the centre of the wall beneath the window and invited the doctors and nurses to leave via an adjoining door. One of the security team had changed quickly into a doctor's outfit, with a concealed baton beneath his cloak, and the other had found a chair beside the door, on high alert and well aware he was likely to be a target as well. They were prepared for an ingress through the door or, more likely, via the window. But they had not accounted for the maintenance hatch in the ceiling above them.

Two doctors and three nurses came through a low door, a door which neither Trey nor the girl had yet noticed.

"We had it covered," one of the security guards grinned at Trey as he dusted himself down, recognising him as one of the otherworld teenagers.

"Didn't look like it to me." Trey gave him a wry smile.

"A girl was hardly going to be a match for us."

At this, the girl grunted and wriggled even harder against her bonds.

"Why...aren't you...dead yet?" She directed her thinly veiled rage at Xci1 in between breaths.

The other guard laughed.

"Because he's not Xci1. That's an actor. The real Xci1 is safe in the tramway beneath the Summer Palace."

The girl's jaw dropped.

"You're wrong," she said. "Everyone knows the face of Xci1."

"Remove your mask, my man," said the guard dressed as a nurse. "Show her how perfect it is."

The actor coloured a little and then coughed.

"In fact," he said, with an almost apologetic smile and unmistakeable voice. "The girl is correct. I am Xci1." There was a stupefied silence. "It is the actor who is safely in the tramway beneath the Summer Palace."

There were big intakes of breath.

"What?"

"Of course you're not..."

"No, the plan was..."

But Xci1 raised his hands.

"I was completely in agreement with the plan apart from one thing – there was no way I was going to let someone put their life on the line for me like that." He looked at Trey. "So, with help, I switched places with the actor, and it ended up working perfectly. Everyone at the palace, including the assassin, thought I was the real deal and all the security personnel thought I was an actor, otherwise they never would have gone along with the plan."

"You let him do this?" one guard said to Trey, his eyes wide. Trey nodded. After half an hour of weathering Xci1's fiery rebuttals during the planning, Trey had realised with a sinking heart what the others hadn't – that the only way to make the plan happen was to allow Xci1's deception and to pray to Xcion that he would be safe. So Trey had been the one to help him concoct this misdirection. And Trey had been in the motorcade when, at a crossroads, the car stopped over an access point to the tramway and the masked actor descended and Xci1 ascended through a small hatch into the car.

"I was wearing a second graphene mask and another set of body armour," Xci1 continued. "Just as my stand-in had done. Thankfully, the bullet only knocked me out for a couple of minutes."

The girl, who hadn't stopped wrestling against her bonds, snarled from the corner of the room.

"You didn't fool me," she spat. "I always knew you were Xci1."

Xci1 smiled.

"Sure," he said. "Okay, let's get her over to a secure place at the Summer Palace." He spoke to the guard next to him who had straightened his back since realising there was real royalty in the room. "Tomorrow, we'll make it known that we have caught the assassin alive, and that we're going to transfer her at noon to a different facility, this time in Tsarn."

"You'll never get me to talk," the girl said. "You can do what you like to me, but I'll never talk."

"That may be true. But your employers don't know that, do they? A few well-chosen words in the morning bulletin should do the trick."

"But," the girl's voice was flat, "they'll send someone to kill me."

"Since you have attempted to kill me and have killed at least four others, I don't see why that should concern me," Xci1 responded.

"I've failed my mission, and I knew the risks." Her face was blank. "You should know, though, whoever they send for me won't spare anyone. You've leapt from the frying pan into the fire, Xci1."

"Well, we'll see," the weary Xci1 responded.

And with that, the little group moved out to a waiting motorcade. The girl was bundled into a police van and moved into a secure cell at the Summer Palace. Then Marcia drove Xci1, Max, Trey and Zika back to Arelard in a tram.

19

A Booking

Once the assassin was captured, Kia decided she needed a break from XSHC. She left through the main door thinking she might wander around the castle and see what had changed over the past century or so. But as the door closed behind her, a little golden circle appeared, grew rapidly, engulfed her, and she found herself back in her room at her desk in England.

As she sat down and the events in Anasius faded away, the reality of her own situation rushed in upon her with the force of an express train. She picked up her phone from the desk where she had dropped it and prepared to message Jason. She started typing a few times but deleted every attempt. She sat forwards in her chair, her elbows on the desk, and allowed herself a little cry.

It turned out to be a long cry. And sometimes she thought she was done with crying, but then it came over her again. She felt caught in a hurricane, anchorless, blown about without anything solid to grasp. Her stomach somersaulted here and there for no apparent reason, making her feel nauseous. For the hundredth time she asked herself how she had allowed herself to get into this position. She remembered the counsellor at school, and the conversations they had had – conversations which had seemed so rational and sensible and matter of fact. She needed matter of fact. She decided to message the counsellor, and to her surprise she received an almost immediate response.

Minutes later, she and the counsellor were talking on the phone. Kia confirmed the decision she had made before, but she still refused to tell her parents.

"This is *my* problem, and *I'm* going to handle it," she said fiercely.

"Of course," the counsellor responded. "But often people need support afterwards, and usually the best people to provide that are the people closest to you."

"If my parents find out, they will kill me," Kia said flatly, almost believing it herself. She didn't see that her parents needed to know. They would be devastated and disappointed and angry and every other emotion that would make it harder for her just to live her life moving forwards. No, them not knowing was by far the easiest way. And so the counsellor accepted her decision as she was legally obligated to do. But she did urge Kia to take someone with her the following day and not try to cope alone. Kia was noncommittal but thanked her for the help. The conversation was over.

A few moments later, her whirling thoughts returned to Jason. She wanted to explain it to him, to make him understand. She had huge plans for her future – university, a high-powered career...She was not even seventeen, and this would ruin everything for her unless she dealt with it.

"It's *my* body," she thought to herself, shaking her head at the messages Jason had sent her the night before. "It's all very well for him to say what he thinks, but he's not in my position. It doesn't affect him." The clinic was booked for the following day, and after that everything could go back to normal. She felt a flood of relief as she considered it. Maybe it would be best not to tell Jason.

But as soon as she had the thought, she tensed. She didn't want to alienate him – he was too important to her. She knew that now. She would tell him sometime, of course, but should she tell him before the event? That was the key question. Marcia would usually help her with decisions like this, but she knew Marcia was on Jason's side on this issue. The hurricane in her head and the churning in her stomach continued. She was utterly alone.

Then she wiped her hands across her face and stood up. "Coffee," she thought to herself firmly. "You need coffee." And she left her room and headed downstairs to find one. She stopped by the bathroom – she seemed to get sick quite a lot these days. Then she spent a bit of time washing her face and sorting her makeup, so she looked less like she'd spent the last hour crying.

By the time the coffee was in her hand, it seemed less appealing, but she carried it back upstairs anyway, glad her parents were snoozing in the lounge. And then, just as her thoughts were beginning to turn back to XSHC, the assassin and all that had happened in Anasius, she reached for her phone and felt the surge of electricity. She was extracted once again.

20

Infiltration

Kia found herself back in the corridor at what could have been the same moment she had left it – there was no way of knowing. She moved to the nearby bathroom, checked her face and decided to return to XSHC. "Maybe I won't even make it back to England for my appointment at the clinic anyway," she thought. As she re-entered the room, she saw the girl assassin being frog-marched into City Hall to face a quick trial before a judge and then her exile to Tsarn. The girl looked pale and tired, but no less determined than she had been when she was first captured. But Kia's attention was caught by Jason and Joe about to move out to begin their mission to infiltrate Turonia.

"Remember," Xci1 said, putting a hand on Joe's shoulder and looking at both boys, "plant the listening devices and find out as much as you can: whether they train assassins, who our captive is, and what Turonia's plan for future invasions might be. But please be careful, this is just a reconnaissance mission after all."

Nodding, Joe opening the door to leave.

"Are you sure you want to do this?" Kia made one last plea, her eyes brushing Jason's. His response was a brief, awkward kiss on the cheek.

"Not in here, idiot," Joe admonished him as they exited the room. Jason reddened, but the deed was done, and various security personnel were smirking as they turned back to their screens.

With that, Joe and Jason took the tram to City Hall at Port Diblaine where they were met by a small team who had prepared their equipment and walked with them down to the quayside.

Jason surveyed the scene and bit his lip. Unlike Joe, he had taken some persuasion to join the mission into the Order of the Dragon, mostly due to thoughts of Kia and the niggling awareness that he wasn't as fit as he once was. But Xci1's desperation and Joe's enthusiasm had won him over. Anasius needed them. Joe was always up for an adventure, he took the view that everything "would be alright on the night," whereas Jason had grown a little more circumspect after his previous experiences in Anasius. Now, as they prepared to leave, the risks loomed large for Jason.

What if they didn't make it across the sea? What if their little submarine couldn't power upstream in a river that turned out to be too fast-flowing? What if they couldn't find a way into the compound from the river? What if they made it into the Order of the Dragon compound but then discovered that the OOD was basically just a boarding school for orphans, and not a training camp for assassins? What if they were caught in the compound? What if they were tortured, or killed? Try as he might, the questions piled up in his mind and he had to fight them to overcome the sense of panic that was bubbling in him. Unbeknown to him, Kia had similar worries back at XSHC. If Jason didn't make it...Kia swallowed as she thought about it. She did not want the last communication between her and Jason to be a disagreement.

In the early evening light, Jason and Joe were kitted out in full wetsuits and given their Scrolls.

"These will guide you when it seems like all else is lost," the elderly man had said as he'd pressed the Scrolls into their hands. Jason looked at the credit-card-like black rectangle in his palm and felt a surge of warmth. From experience, he knew, without a doubt, that the man was right. He pressed it into an A4 shape and watched as the foldable screen glowed into action. Something about having it in his hand made him feel stronger. He clipped it onto his drybag.

As they packed into the tiny underwater vessel at Port Diblaine, Kia could only watch from the screens at XSHC. The vessel reminded Jason of Will and Maylin's new "turtle" back in Juntaou, except that it was far more advanced – 200 years' worth of technological advancement had seen to that. It was also fully enclosed, rather than dragging its occupants through the water as they clung to the top. The craft seemed to be constructed half in steel and half in glass. It had a broad window on its base through which they could see the riverbed a few feet below, a wide curving glass edge all around, and a sort of glass dome which formed the roof. It also had a much longer range on its battery, searchlights recessed into the body, a virtually silent engine, and a state-of-the-art navigation system.

As the boys settled into the craft, three drybags were stowed carefully beside them, and they were given their final instructions before closing the hatch.

"Let's go!" Joe cried, pushing a lever downwards as the navigation screen sprung into life in front of their faces. Joe took command of the controls, steering the craft with his hands and adjusting the speed with his feet. Jason sat behind, happy to navigate.

They were travelling a few feet below the surface, barely rippling the water as they moved out of the port into the Dagon River. Jason reminded Joe to turn north so they could get out of the estuary and into Mannasa Sound, and ten minutes later, they were leaving Anasius behind and crossing the northern sea towards Turonia.

Some miles out from Anasius, there was a soft bump to the vehicle.

"What was that?" Joe broke the silence.

But he had hardly finished the question when a large shadowy shape crossed just above them, and another flashed across in front of them. Dolphins, they realised at the same time. Joe slowed the craft, but it didn't matter. The playful beasts were clearly very interested, crowding in for a closer look. They were diving and jumping and circling around the craft, occasionally nosing it with their funny-looking snouts. It was a bumpy ride.

"Maybe we could outrun them?" Joe pushed the accelerator lever on his left foot all the way to the back.

The craft leapt forward, climbing up to an impressive twenty-one knots, but despite travelling at what felt like a crazy speed, the dolphins continued to swim around them. Worrying that they might crash into something, Joe pedalled back on the accelerator, and they slowed to a less terrifying pace. It was another couple of miles before the dolphins lost interest and swam away.

The remainder of the journey was uneventful until the last few miles. Four miles out, they had to turn their external navigation system off to avoid detection from Turonian shipping, so now they were travelling by sight alone. Joe was trying to watch both ahead and beneath them – he didn't want to ground them on the sea floor. Jason was looking to the sides, turning his head this way and that as he tried to make sure he could warn Joe of any obstacles.

As they approached Turonia, the sea floor rose rapidly beneath them and Jason cried out for Joe to slow the craft. Within moments, the little craft was sliding along just below the surface as they hunted for the entrance to the river that led down to the compound of the Order of the Dragon.

It was not easy to find. They tried to hug the coastline, moving just a couple of feet below the waves which flowed in to break on Turonia's shingle shores. Jason and Joe followed the contours of the seafloor, moving in and out of every inlet in the hope it would lead to the river. It was extremely slow progress. Suddenly, their implants burst to life.

"Guys, what have you been doing?" It was crackling – they were a considerable distance from Anasius – but it was unmistakable. It was Kia from XSHC at Arelard Castle.

"First you slowed to a crawling pace, then you pushed the sub to its maximum speed and were in danger of overheating the engine. And now you're nearly a mile east of where you should be."

"How can we possibly be a mile out? We were bang on target until we had to turn off our navigation." Joe was puzzled.

"The current," Jason said simply. "There must be a strong current running west to east along the coast. When our navigation system was running, the sub adjusted for current automatically, but without it, we were always going to drift. How have you managed to reach us all the way out here, Kia?"

"We're piggybacking off a Turonian satellite. We had to hack the encryption system and it was rather more complex than we thought it would be, but we succeeded. And I'm confident the Turonians will never notice."

Joe manoeuvred away from the shoreline and sped up to nine knots.

A few minutes later, he asked, "Kia, surely we're nearly at the river by now?"

Her voice came back in the implants, "You're still about one hundred metres from the river mouth, but it'll feel more like one hundred and fifty with the current you're fighting. Just be careful once you turn into the river. You'll be moving out of the cross-current and into an estuary. We have no idea how fast that river is running, or how shallow it might be. I'll update you as soon as you get there."

Joe angled the craft back towards the shore, and a couple of minutes later they found what looked like yet another inlet. As they followed it around, they realised this must be the river mouth, so they moved away from the right-hand bank and then eased forwards, testing the strength of the current by keeping the bank in their vision and observing how quickly it moved past their line of sight.

Eventually they saw the remains of a pier ahead which they had to navigate around, and then a bridge across the river a hundred metres later. They settled back to travel at a walking pace. They didn't want to break the submarine and be stranded in Turonia.

"Great going, guys," Kia's voice came over their implants again, with biting sarcasm. "At that pace, you should get to the compound by first light tomorrow."

"If we go much faster, we won't get there at all," Joe retorted. "There are loads of obstacles, fish, piers, bridges, ever-changing riverbanks and river depth, and we're struggling to see any of it. Any faster and we'll crash into something, and the mission will be over before it's even started."

"Keep going like this and you're going to be another hour and it'll be totally dark by then," Kia pleaded. "You won't be able to see the compound wall without using your searchlights, and they could expose you to the Order of the Dragon guards. Why don't I direct you? I suspect that craft is built well enough to withstand any fish."

"You suspect?" It was Joe's turn to be sarcastic. "There's no chance we could die by unexpected fish splat?"

Jason laughed despite himself. There was silence from the implants.

Nevertheless, Joe squeezed down on the accelerator pedal, pushing their speed up to nearly nine knots, raising the craft so that it was travelling only a foot below the surface – they wanted as much water as possible between them and the riverbed. Kia's instructions via the implants kept them in or near the middle of the river, but it was still terrifying to be flying along underwater unable to see much and not knowing whether they were about to crash into a bridge.

After ten minutes, Kia's directions became faint.

"The river's now only ten metres wide...don't know how deep...careful and...eyes peeled," she instructed. "About fifty metres...before...khsssss...on your right...ssshhhh... maybe ninety second...sswshkksshhh."

"Hello?" Joe said. But static had swallowed her voice.

"Looks like we're on our own now, Joe," Jason swallowed. "Watch out for the riverbed, it's getting pretty shallow."

Joe slowed the craft even more and manoeuvred towards the right bank. Jason spotted the riverbed below them and shouted a warning. Joe slowed even further until they were virtually crawling forwards. The next two minutes felt like an eternity.

And then, without any warning, the riverbed dropped away like a cliff.

"I'm guessing there's a channel into the compound," Joe said. "We need to turn right and sink lower in the water; we don't want to be spotted."

He eased them down until they were five feet under, wondering how they would know when they had reached the compound.

They didn't have long to wait. A few moments later there was a solid wall in front of them, and to their right, they could see the foot of a ladder, stretching up to the surface. Jason felt a shiver fall down his spine. They had arrived. Joe pushed the diving lever and drove the craft carefully downwards until it hovered just a metre above the riverbed. Then he cut the engine and they began to drift upwards and forwards slightly, soon bumping gently into the wall in front of them.

"Right," he murmured. "This is where the fun begins." The boys were on high alert, nerves jangling and pulses racing. They were about to infiltrate an utterly unknown compound full of highly trained fighters. The whole idea seemed insane.

They prepared themselves to swim out of the submarine and across to the ladder. If they had opened the top hatch, the air in the sub would have escaped, filling the sub with water, sinking it and pushing a huge air bubble to the surface, making their presence known to anyone who may have been there. So, instead, they planned to exit the submarine covertly.

They grabbed the three drybags, donned diving goggles, turned on the head torches, checked the snorkels were attached and within reach, and then carefully opened the hatch underneath them. Jason took a few huge gulps of air and dived into the murky water, swimming away from the hatch and making way for Joe to follow. Swiftly, he made his way around to the front of the craft, located the tether-hook, unreeled it, and attached one of the two dumbbells they had brought, dropping it to the side of the craft next to the front wall. Joe had followed him almost immediately, and he attached the second dumbbell as planned. Theoretically, now the submarine would neither drift up to the surface nor back down the river.

Jason and Joe moved together upwards through the water, following the ladder as they went. Jason was increasingly desperate for oxygen, but dared not let any bubbles slip from his mouth for fear he would meet someone at the top. Snorkel at the ready, he rose up and prepared to break the surface. Would his gasp for air be his final breath?

21

The Belly of the Beast

Across from the guards' office, the water lapped quietly at the dock just across from the open door. In the late evening sunshine, the camouflage netting high above the water cast dappled shadows on the surface. Laughter was floating out of the room as three guards discussed the antics of a junior trainee during the day. They had disciplined him appropriately as they were trained to do, but now they could not help but see the funny side. One of them was standing, his brown robe slung over a nearby chair. He had a short, yellow-handled knife strapped to his right thigh, within easy reach of his fingers, his dark brown eyes scanned the series of screens in from of him and he was grinning as he remembered the antics. Then he glanced at the clock and lost the smile.

"Only a few more minutes, gents, and then we'll need to do the lock-up rounds. Please remember to sign everything off before you are relieved and turn in for the night – failure to do that requires our night staff to repeat your locking-up process all over again."

“Yeah, yeah, we know,” complained another guard, sitting at a monitor and tapping away at the keys. A third guard was lounging in a chair with his feet up on a desk, engrossed in a screen he held on his lap. His shoes were off and he rubbed his temples as he read. It was clear that he hadn’t heard a word that had been said.

Outside, Jason and Joe broke the surface, taking deep breaths of air and removing their goggles as quietly as they could. They gazed around and realised they were virtually in the direct line of sight of the guard with his feet up. They sank back down below the surface again and swam towards the dockside, terrified they had been seen. They surfaced again and looked around. Now they were on the nearer side of the dock and out of the sightline of the guards’ room.

The smart wooden dock was beautifully built in dark treated oak, and it wrapped around the end of the inlet, running for perhaps ten or twelve metres down each side as well. The ladder they had used to swim up to the surface was the only ladder from the dock into the water, but along each side were four bollards regularly spaced, presumably for mooring boats. Clearly the deck was built to accommodate much larger vessels than the little submarine the boys had arrived in. People could then step easily from vessel to the deck and vice versa.

From where the boys were treading water, the inlet had vertical concrete sides which rose up perhaps a metre from the water to the wooden deck. In other words, unless the boys used the ladder, getting out of the water was going to be extremely difficult. But the top of the ladder was front and centre to the view from the guards' room.

Even if they could somehow launch themselves out of the water high enough to grab the dockside and haul themselves over, it would be a very noisy event and was bound to attract attention. At the same time, treading water could not be sustained. And anyone who walked out had only to glance into the water and they would be seen. The seconds ticked by.

Joe signalled to Jason to put on their masks and snorkels. Then he sank beneath the surface and swam away from the dockside, heading back towards the river. Jason wondered what Joe had in mind, but since he couldn't think of any better idea, he decided to trust his friend and follow.

Joe had stopped at the end of the wooden dock. Here there was a steel mesh running from the outer edge of the compound wall down to the dockside like a giant curtain. It was bolted into the ceiling, the side wall and the concrete floor beneath the dock, as well as sticking out about a foot into the inlet and travelling right to the bottom of the river. If they emerged from the inlet beyond the steel mesh, there would be no way into the compound at all because the steel mesh prevented access. Joe pointed upwards and then surfaced, Jason acting in sync. They removed their snorkels and looked back to the dock and security office.

"This has got to be our way out," Joe whispered. But before he could explain further, two guards emerged from the office. Jason and Joe grabbed each other, took a breath and sank back beneath the water, waiting with hammering hearts for the guards to move on and wishing they had not removed their snorkels.

One guard crossed the dock and entered a door on the opposite side, which he then closed behind him. The second guard scanned the dockside and stared down the water towards the river. If Jason and Joe had been above the surface then, they would have been seen. But they were not. Joe, an experienced swimmer, was calculating that they could stay down no more than another thirty seconds, but Jason was already running out of oxygen.

Suddenly, Jason had no choice. He shook his head and surfaced, gasping in air as quietly as he could. Joe followed him, fixing his eyes on the dock to see if any of the guards were still present. The guard who had been staring at the water was now walking directly away and out into the open ground of the compound itself. Joe and Jason drew a collective sigh of relief.

Seeing the steel mesh and remembering what Joe had said, he asked, "What did you mean?"

Joe just grinned and pointed at it. It was getting dark, but as Joe squinted harder towards the mesh, he understood. It was designed to keep intruders out but also made a perfect ladder from the water. The lads could use it to climb out and onto the end of the dock. Feeling fatigued and not knowing when the guards might return, they put the idea into action right away. A minute later, they were standing on the end of the dock holding their drybags. They were dripping, cold and out of breath, but they had made it this far.

Before doing anything else, they got themselves out of their wetsuits and into the dry, black camouflage gear they had brought in one of the drybags. They stowed the bag with their wetsuits, masks and snorkels behind an abandoned crate next to the steel mesh, hoping no-one would find it.

Suddenly, strong dazzling downlights flooded the whole dock in light. The office door, the odd pieces of rope, the life rings, the ladder and the dock itself were thrown into sharp relief. The light fell all the way to the steel curtain, leaving the lads nowhere to hide. They had no option but to move swiftly and silently down the dockside towards the security office, hoping it was unoccupied.

As they approached the doorway, Joe dropped quietly to the floor and crawled forwards, preparing to glance around the open doorway from a few inches off the floor. Jason stood a couple of feet behind him and waited.

And then their fears materialised. They heard noises near the inside of the door before a guard emerged through the doorway. He sensed their presence and looked up. Jason stared at him. Their eyes met as the guard's right hand dropped to his side to get his weapon.

On the floor, in those brief moments before the guard noticed him, Joe reacted to the situation without even thinking. He grabbed the guard's legs and squeezed them together, at the same time pushing into him with his right shoulder. It was a classic rugby move he knew from school. The guard started to cry out as he crashed to the floor, but he hit his head on a bollard on his way down and the noise died away.

Jason rushed past the guard to the doorway of the office and peered inside, terrified they would soon have other guards to deal with. Much to his relief, the office was empty. Jason looked down at Joe, who was releasing the guard's legs. He was out cold. They both listened hard. Surely someone else heard the noise.

But as the moments passed, they could hear nothing at all except their own breathing, and they realised that, impossibly, they had got away with it. Jason felt a wash of awe at his friend's quick thinking, soon followed by a twinge of jealousy. Why hadn't he acted like that?

"What now?" Jason whispered. "We can't leave him there."

"I dunno, but let's at least tie him up so we won't have to fight him when he comes round."

They retrieved some of the lengths of rope scattered on the dock and tied the guard's legs together and his arms behind his back. Jason found a rag on a shelf in the security office. He stuffed it into the guard's mouth and tied it in place with another piece of rope. When the guard came to, he would be unable to move or make a noise.

"Where can we put him?" Jason asked.

They checked over the security office. Most of it was open plan, with screens and computers sprinkled around it. There were a couple of large plants, a sofa and a coffee table in one corner, also affording nowhere to hide an unconscious guard. Jason saw two doors on the far wall of the office, opposite the door onto the dock. He ran across to check them.

He tested the first door, finding that it swung outwards and opened onto a brightly lit and thankfully empty corridor. It didn't look hopeful. He tested the second, but it wouldn't open. He wanted to reach for his Scroll but remembered that Turonians didn't have them, so it wouldn't work on these locked doors. From across the room, Joe held up the keys the guard had been fumbling with. He tested various keys before finding one that worked. And it was worth the effort. The door swung open to reveal a cleaning cupboard, with shelves down one wall carrying cloths, bottles of labelled cleaning fluids and so on. The cupboard was not huge, but was easily large enough to stow a trussed-up security guard.

Jason and Joe ran back and managed to carry the guard from the dock, through the office, to the cupboard. They pushed him inside, propping him up against the back wall. Then they closed the door, locked it and Joe pocketed the keys. All of a sudden, the lights on the dock went out again.

"It seems like the lights only come on when there's movement on the dock," Jason noticed. Joe agreed. The boys looked at each other, feeling as if they could breathe easily for the first time since they'd entered the compound. Jason felt his body ache with tiredness, but he straightened up. They had a job to do.

"This is probably a good place for our first listening device," he said.

Joe nodded. Jason unzipped one of the drybags and removed a little tin box. Inside were five small black buttons, each one a tiny microphone with a powerful transmitter and a battery life of around twenty-four hours. He removed one and looked around the room, eventually sticking it to the underside corner of one of the desk drawers. No-one would ever find it.

The office was not particularly interesting. There were the usual office desks and chairs scattered about, each with a large screen but no visible keyboard. It was windowless, with light coming from the overhead downlights and from the standing lamps near the sofa. What was interesting was the fact that the long left-hand wall seemed to be one enormous screen, divided up into one large, wide section at the top and six smaller sections beneath. Each part of the screen showed in real time various locations across the compound, both outside in the large courtyard but also in the various buildings around.

The outside camera views flicked between satellite imagery to footage from the cameras mounted in the eaves of the buildings. They scrolled through the seven images, lingering perhaps ten seconds on each image before moving to the next one. Even though it was dark, the images were still relatively clear – the cameras obviously had some kind of night vision.

But before Jason and Joe could take an in-depth look at the lay of the land, they heard the unmistakable "crunching" of boots walking towards them.

"Quick," Jason whispered, dashing across to the door that led into the corridor. They both slipped through. Joe fished out the keys and tried three before he found the one that fitted. He locked the door as quietly as he could.

“That might slow him down a little bit.” Joe took off after Jason down the corridor.

22

A Narrow Escape

Jason and Joe found themselves in a white-walled corridor with various doors. Not knowing what they might find behind each door, they ran instinctively, only stopping just before the double doors at the end. They listened hard and, from the door they had locked, heard the distinctive sound of keys going into the keyhole.

"No choice!" Joe panted, pushing at the double doors. They opened into the lower end of an auditorium. There was a wide, deep stage area just below them to their left, with black curtains either side of the stage and a huge screen on the back wall. Plush, red tiered seating ran up from the stage in ascending rows, with steps at each side and a slope down the central ascending aisle. Thankfully the auditorium was devoid of people, but as the lights were low, it had taken their eyes a few seconds to adjust to the dimness. They hovered about unsure what to do, but they were galvanised into action by the sound of the security guard in the corridor they had occupied only moments before.

Spotting the little door at the top of the auditorium, the lads ran lightly up the steps and Jason tried the handle. It opened easily enough, onto a spiral staircase that ran upwards from the auditorium. They slipped through, closing the door behind them. Now they couldn't hear anything, either from the corridor where the security guard had been or from up the staircase before them. Joe slipped the keys from his pocket again and worked his way through them as he tried to lock the small door they'd just entered through. A minute later he located the correct one and managed to lock the door behind them – now they would know if anyone was coming.

Meanwhile, Jason had climbed the stairs, as quickly and quietly as he could. At the top, the staircase opened up into a small room with a large window overlooking the stage area of the auditorium below. There was long wide desk running below the window, holding a computer terminal, three large screens, a touchpad labelled "lighting" and another labelled "acoustics". Some shelving lined the back wall, laden with speakers, folded blackout curtains, cables, spotlights of various sizes, colour filters, and little electronic boxes which looked like remote controls. As he peered into the room, Jason realised two things. First, it was empty. Second, it was a dead end. They had trapped themselves.

He bounded back down the stairs.

"It's a dead end," Jason whispered loudly. "It's just the tech room for the auditorium." Joe winced at his volume and gesticulated for him to be quieter.

"But there has to be a way out," Joe whispered fiercely again, running swiftly up the staircase to see for himself, pulling himself up by the curving balustrade as he took two or three steps at a time. Jason followed him up. For the second time, he stared around the room, and Joe did the same. There were definitely no other doors, and the window to the auditorium was fixed glass. Then, almost simultaneously, they spotted the answer: a skylight.

It was about two feet by three feet, recessed high into the ceiling above them and, most important of all, it had what looked like a catch at one end, suggesting it was possible to open it. But how? And how far would it open?

They found various switches and began pushing them to see what would happen. Jason tried one and the whole room got bathed in light. Joe cried out and Jason pushed it off again immediately. They held their breath, listened hard, and stared down into the darkened auditorium, desperately hoping no-one was there. A few seconds later, they allowed themselves to breathe again.

"Sorry," Jason said as Joe frowned at him.

"This might do it," Joe said after a few minutes of rooting around. He handed Jason a remote control he'd found on a shelf to the left of the main auditorium window. "But it doesn't seem to work."

Jason took it from him and, as he examined the remote, his finger touched the rectangle on its surface. Instantly, there was a faint whirring sound and the whole skylight seemed to quiver. But nothing else happened. He tried touching it again, this time holding his finger on the rectangle. The result was the same. Then he tried swiping his finger down the pad. And when he did, slowly but surely, the skylight slid smoothly into the roof cavity, disappearing from view. Jason swiped his finger up on the rectangle and the skylight slid back into place.

It was the perfect place to hide. The roof was out of the way of wandering security guards, trainers and students. And it was a vantage point which might help them plan the next few hours. Perhaps from the roof they could figure out the best way to gather the information they needed for XSHC in Anasius. But they needed to get up there.

Jason pulled the desk chair out. "Maybe this?" He set it under the opening.

"It's too far up." Joe shook his head.

But Jason ignored him. Joe, who had led every part of this expedition so far, had every good idea. It was Joe who had driven the submarine, Joe who had found the mesh ladder, Joe who had taken out the guard and now Joe who had found the remote. Now it was Jason's turn. Jason readjusted his position and eyed up the distance. Despite himself, he knew Joe was right – this was going to need a huge leap. Telling a protesting Joe to hold his chair, he barely waited two seconds before crouching and springing towards the hole. But his scrabbling fingers failed to find a hold.

The chair skittered out from under Jason's weight, and he crashed to the floor. His left foot rolled over on his ankle, and he clutched at it, wincing.

"Aah…" he breathed.

"I told you." Joe punched him in the shoulder.

Jason was in too much pain to notice.

Joe frowned as he pulled out their very minimal first-aid kit from his drybag. It contained an assortment of skin plasters (an Anasiun invention that stopped bleeding and provided synthetic skin cells to speed up healing time), pain medication, and an eye dressing. He looked around for a better first-aid kit in the tech room, but instead, his eyes fell on the blackout curtains. He got up off the floor and fetched one. It turned out to be quite huge, so he found a frayed bit near one end and tore off a long strip of fabric. The noise felt deafening, but Joe had given up worrying too much about noise. He went to Jason, offered him some pain relief, and suggested they bind up the ankle a bit whilst they figured out what to do. Now what hope did they have of getting out of the skylight?

A few minutes later, both boys were sitting down. Joe was slumped against the wall and Jason was on the desk chair with his foot bound up and resting up on the desk. He was feeling a bit better, but his ankle – and his pride – hurt. A lot. There would be no more jumping off the chairs. He had spotted a broom leaning against the wall in the corner and fashioned it into a half-decent crutch by wrapping some curtain fabric around the head so he could put it under his left armpit.

"You'll have to go without me," Jason said with a weak grin.

"I'm sure the Turonians will take you in as one of their own," Joe agreed. "Sounds like they're well known for their hospitality."

"Yeah, it's a good thing they're not trained killers or anything."

"You'll be alright, you've got your broom."

Neither boy could resist laughing at that.

"Don't be an idiot," Joe said, standing up. "You're coming with me."

Even though they'd been joking, Jason felt a twinge of relief. Being wounded in the heart of enemy territory was not a pleasant predicament. For a brief second, he was glad the implants weren't working. Kia wouldn't have to know.

Joe interrupted him. "Let's make this remaining curtain into a rope. I can take it up to the roof with me by climbing on those shelves and hoisting myself up."

Jason felt a prickle of heat in his cheeks as he looked at the shelves. That would have been a far better first option.

"You can tie things on the end of it to make sure we take whatever we need," Joe continued. "Then put the chair under the desk, make sure the room's in order, and grab onto the rope and I'll pull you up."

"You'll pull me up?" Jason repeated.

"Yeah. I'm strong and fit. Unlike you," he added.

Jason let the jibe go.

They fashioned a rope by tearing a curtain into strips and then plaiting and knotting the strips together. It took them back to the first time they'd ever learnt to do this at the beginning of their training in the Overlord Academy. Joe removed the two largest speakers from the lowest shelf, positioned them below the skylight and then helped Jason to a standing position on top of them, leaning on the upturned broom. Then he climbed the shelves and stepped out onto Jason's shoulders. It took four attempts before Joe finally managed to get high enough to grasp the outer edge of the roofing. He hauled his weight up through the hole until his top half was lying across the roof's smooth hard surface. He wriggled and kicked, found a grip with his feet, and pushed himself completely through the hole. As he was climbing, Jason sank back onto the chair for a moment to give his ankle some respite – it was throbbing horribly. He would have done anything for stronger painkillers. After a minute or so, he forced himself to get up. He hobbled and struggled and puffed and panted to replace the speakers on the shelves. Then he stuffed another curtain plus the remnants of the first one into one of the drybags, removed all evidence of their presence and pushed the chair back under the desk.

Joe looked around in the darkness of the late evening. The roof sloped down gently from his position. The hole from the skylight was just above him on the upward slope, and a couple of metres above that was a ridgeline beyond which he could not see. But for the occasional outlet pipes of some sort sticking out of the roof, and a few other skylights, the roof looked like it ran smooth and unbroken across the whole length and breadth of the building. Swiftly, he untied from his waist the curtain rope they had made and dangled the end through the hole. Jason was waiting for him.

After sending the broom and two drybags up to Joe, it was Jason's turn. He pocketed the remote control, zipped his pocket up, and grasped hold of the end of the rope which was dangling once again through the hole. He put his legs through the two loops Joe had made, trying to ignore all the pain in his ankle, and grasped the rope above him with both hands.

Up on the roof, Joe stood, facing away from the hole, and leant slightly down the slope as he did so. "Looks like all that gym time is going to be worth it," he thought to himself. This had to work. The makeshift rope went tight. Joe pulled.

Unable to lift Jason by hand, Joe had decided to brace his feet and lean forward, applying all his weight forwards on the rope and away from the hole. And by some miracle, he managed to take some steps down the roof incline. Inside, Jason rose upwards in short jerks, worrying whether the rope would fray against the edge of the roof. As soon as he was high enough, he grasped the edge of the roof as Joe had done before him and pulled hard to get up through the hole. In fact, he did such a good job of taking his own weight on his arms that, with the weight on the rope suddenly dwindling to almost nothing, Joe nearly fell. He stumbled a couple of steps forward before managing to regain his balance. Jason was now out of the skylight.

Panting, Jason twisted around so he could see back into the hole. He swiped downwards on the remote, took aim, and threw it through the open skylight towards the crumpled-up curtain under the little shelf. The remote landed right on target as the skylight slid noiselessly shut. Hopefully, no-one would have any idea the lads had been there.

23

Confusion

Chines was feeling increasingly more inadequate, even as second-in-command. He had hunted for this assassin for weeks, imagining all kinds of things about him, but now he discovered the assassin was no more than a young teenage girl. How had he, a highly trained and, so he had thought, highly intelligent officer at XSHC missed the fact that the assassin was a child? And how had these teenagers who had come from another world – if the Xcis were to be believed – succeeded where he had failed?

He had watched the video footage from Ducal City and Xanver over and over again and spotted nothing. These youngsters had watched the same footage five or six times, and then, somehow, Trey had seen the same small figure in both sets of images. How had Chines missed it? And then the teenagers had come together and figured out an audacious plan to keep Xci1 safe *and* to capture the assassin at one and the same time. Then they had carried out the plan, with feet on the ground in the face of great danger in a country not their own, and with direction and instruction from

Kia back at XSHC. They had succeeded, and the assassin was in custody.

He was even more certain now than before that he was not the man for the top job, and it was a relief to him that he was not in charge. Later, as he pulled out the small unfolding bed from the wall, he wondered whether he might as well go home. Kia seemed far better at the job than he was anyway. He tossed and turned, wondering about the teenagers in Turonia and trying hard to figure out how to make contact with them. He drifted off to sleep.

*

Xci1, Trey, Max and Zika had returned to Arelard Castle with Marcia. And at XSHC itself, Kia had been engrossed in two things. As well as supporting Joe and Jason's mission into the Order of the Dragon, she was also working on a way to draw Turonia out into the open. The five friends were crowded round a desk in the middle of the room, deep in conversation with Xci1.

"We need somewhere public but not crowded. Somewhere seemingly innocuous and not far from the Notalian border to make it easy for Turonia to get to," Kia was saying. "Come on Marcia – you're the geography genius."

"Well, Ducal City is close to the Notalian border," Marcia responded. "But I think it's more likely they'll try to get her here at Ruwark as she exits City Hall."

"You're right," Zika chipped in. "They'd only need to get someone across the sea, or they could cross the sea to Parlmoni and then come via the desert to Anasius." He paused. "But isn't this highly risky? I mean, the assassin might just be gunned down. We don't have the personnel to protect her."

"Masks," Trey spoke into the silence that followed. "Could we have a graphene mask made for her overnight? It would protect her, like it protected Your Highness." He bowed to Xci1 as he spoke his name. "And it would help us draw out whomever they send for her. As long as we can persuade Turonia that the assassin is preparing to talk to us, they'll want her out of the picture. Capturing this second assassin is essential. That way we'll definitely find out what Turonia are up to, and they would never be able to deny their attack."

They all looked at Xci1.

"It's a good idea," he said after a pause. "Commissioner?"

The Commissioner started. He was dozing on the wide plush sofa next to the drinks area.

"I'm sorry, Your Highness." He reddened as he realised it was Xci1 who had spoken. He stumbled to his feet and bowed awkwardly. "Can I help?"

Xci1 smiled despite the situation. The Commissioner had never been caught napping in his life before. "Commissioner, how can we organise a graphene mask to be made for a girl in the dungeons at City Hall?"

"Well, we'd have to get her to Juntaou where she can have a fitting like you did. Then we'd have to—"

"—No, you don't understand. We need a graphene mask to be ready to fit onto her tomorrow morning."

"But...but," the Commissioner sputtered. "It's already nearly dark. The two firms will be closed until tomorrow. How can we get her to Juntaou and...?"

Trey spoke again, his brain working at top speed. "Sir, His Royal Highness is asking you for a mask to be ready tomorrow morning."

The group of friends and Xci1 looked at him. The Commissioner's mouth opened and closed three more times. They were asking for the impossible. The graphene linings were made in a lab built into the cliffside by the Dagon River in Juntaou – they could hardly move the whole lab to Ruwark. And masks were constructed from a cast taken from a person's face. If they wanted a mask to fit some girl, the girl would need to be in Juntaou to have a cast taken of her face. And yet here they all stood waiting for him to jump into action. He shook his head.

"I can try."

"Good," Xci1 clapped his hands. "We're counting on you Commissioner. And you can assure our friends in Juntaou that we will compensate them for the trouble."

The Commissioner swallowed and nodded, wishing not for the first time that day that he had a different job.

Kia wasted no time in returning to directing proceedings from her desk in the middle of XSHC. "She really is magnificent," Marcia thought to herself. Even amidst Jason and Joe's mission, Kia was firing off messages to City Hall in Ruwark, jumping up for brief conversations with the Commissioner, and returning to the console to try and talk to Jason and Joe.

The XSHC personnel had avidly watched the journey across the sea and upriver. They had only been able to follow the little black dot on the screen from the tracker mounted in the nose of the submarine. They had heard Kia interact with Jason and Joe and to urge them to move more quickly. Then the communication link had weakened, and eventually died. Now they could neither see nor hear Jason and Joe.

And things had only worsened as Jason and Joe's craft had approached the compound. For some reason, its tracker had failed. They had no idea that it had turned into the inlet and sank to the riverbed, partly because of the tracker failure, but also because the satellite view showed no sign of an inlet. It was carefully hidden by the camouflage netting. In short, XSHC had no idea whether the boys had even made it to the compound.

But after only a few minutes, there had been a ping on the communications panel.

"They made it inside!" one of the officers had exclaimed. "They've just activated one of the listening devices."

But confirming that Jason and Joe were on enemy grounds had done nothing to assuage Kia's nerves.

Twenty minutes later, one of the technicians had zoomed in to a skylight towards the north end of the building by the river. They had watched open-mouthed as Joe emerged through. There was a spontaneous cheer from XSHC, but it died away as they watched Jason being hauled up through the hole. He was obviously injured. Not for the first time that night, Kia had visited the bathroom.

“What’s happening with the sound?” Kia asked for the twelfth time, running her hands through her hair. “Talk to me, Jason,” she thought, as if she could somehow reach him with her mind. She began barking orders, urging everyone to work out what had gone wrong. They had no direct contact with Joe and Jason, and all they could do was watch the little black dot via satellite feed. Kia had a permanent knot in her stomach. She kept the satellite view of the OOD compound up on the large screen that covered the end wall of XSHC, and analysists were watching in real time for movement.

“The problem is that we were piggybacking off their communications satellite with our own encrypted line,” one of the XSHC officers had leaned closer to her to explain. “Not only did we have to encrypt at both ends as usual, but we also had to encrypt up at the satellite. It was the only way to avoid their system from detecting us. As a result, we had to decrypt in two stages at both ends.” Most of the personnel present were nodding their understanding, so Kia nodded as well. It wouldn’t serve the situation at all if they knew she had no idea what he was talking about.

“But then their security system flagged a technical issue so we had to shut it off before they could figure out that we were causing it.”

“So what are you doing about it now?”

The audio technicians looked at one other.

“What about,” Kia stared at the ceiling, thinking hard. She frowned. “I mean, we know that the bugs work, right – the listening devices?”

“Yes…”

“We know that they both receive sound and transmit sound. Is there any way we could transmit to them from here and they receive the sound and send it to Jason and Joe’s implants?”

The three communications technicians looked at each other. You could almost see the cogs turning in their brains. Slowly, they were beginning to nod. Perhaps it would be possible.

“Okay then,” Kia said. “As quickly as you can. Our friends’ lives are at stake.”

24
Losing Count

"Something's off here," Jason frowned.

He and Joe had slithered up to the roofline and were peering over the top, working out the layout of the compound.

As if on cue, the cloud moved away from the moon. It wasn't quite like moving from night to day, but it was certainly very easy to see. Thankfully, with their eyes just above the ridgeline, Jason and Joe were invisible from the compound.

The building on which they lay ran the entire length of the western edge of the compound, and the camouflage netting over the river inlet stretched out a few metres off to their right. At the connection of the western and northern edges lay what looked like a car park. It contained a truck and a strange-looking vehicle – a bit like a quadbike except much larger, with big, heavy-treaded wheels and an enclosed cockpit. Almost level with where the lads were lying, above the car park, was an acre of camouflage netting, protecting the vehicles from the prying eyes of satellites.

Another L-shaped building took up the farther half of the northern boundary and a part of the eastern edge. It was three storeys high and contained evenly spaced windows on the top floors and tall wide windows on the ground floor. There were two double doors into the building, both very plain and business like. Then came a metal-gated archway in the centre of the eastern wall, presumably leading out to the dirt track beyond the compound. The archway was overlooked by a tall, square-shaped guard tower to its right. Beyond that, set out some distance from the wall, was what appeared to be a wide wooden hut with a pitched roof, rather like you might see in our world except that it was much larger. It had various pipes running in and out, and the only windows were tiny narrow ones almost under the eaves. The southern edge of the compound held a fifth building which seemed quite different from the others. Built in a light beige stone, with a wide porch over a grand front entrance and castellations at its roof edge, it could easily have been a stately home for the landed gentry.

They took in the camouflage-coloured razor wire that topped every edge of the compound. They noted the floodlights, standing like silent sentries on the east and west edge of the open area, and the movable spotlights mounted atop the guard tower. They could see various cameras fitted into the eaves of the buildings. By the light recessed into the archway roof, they could see the metal gates below the archway with a keypad, a retinal scanner and an armed guard sitting beneath the overhang. The Order of the Dragon obviously took no chances with security.

The hairs on Jason's neck began to prickle. He still had the distinct impression that something didn't quite fit.

Something was not quite right. He just couldn't put his finger on what it was.

"Looks like a normal compound to me," Joe shrugged. "There are five buildings. I reckon the leaders must live in that grand house. And did you notice the guard tower? I wonder how many guards are in there. A guard tower *and* a security office by the docks. They're certainly not taking any chances, are they...?"

"Oh." A lightbulb turned on in Jason's brain.

"What?" Joe asked.

"There's a guards' office at the river dock; razor wire around the perimeter. But why have a keypad and retinal scan on the inside of the metal gates?"

Joe blinked.

"Because it's not so much that they don't want people to get *in*, but rather that they don't want anyone to get *out*." Jason looked at his friend with bright, excited eyes.

"Yes," Joe breathed in response. "This is more of a prison camp than a training ground. The people who come here..."

"... are prisoners," Jason finished.

This was such a huge shift in their thinking that they were quiet for a few moments, trying to take it in. They remembered Xci1's words about the children taken from their families.

"It's weird though," Joe frowned. "They're ferocious fighters who take great pride in the Order of the Dragon at tournaments. They don't sound like prisoners to me."

At that moment, Jason recalled the frog from biology class. Maybe these fighters had also been deceived. Maybe they also didn't realise they were surrounded by slowly boiling water. Maybe they were too unaware to jump out...

Before he could say as much, he heard a new sound, a bit like a motorbike in the distance, a familiar "chug chug" noise. The noise got louder before they realised it was coming from the river behind them. A boat. It was fast approaching, and they were fully exposed on the roof just above and to the left of the water. All it would take would be for someone on the boat to look up at the roof rather than focusing on the inlet. One little glance and all would be lost. But at that very moment, to their immense relief, the moon disappeared behind a cloud again, plunging them into shadow. Joe thanked his lucky stars. Jason didn't believe in luck.

The boat swung into view, throttled back and headed into the inlet. Then the engine cut out and they could hear splashes and shouts and snippets of conversation drifting up from the dock, along with the sound of items being unloaded. They had no idea how many people there were. A few minutes later, the splashing noises could be heard again and then the chugging of the outboard motor restarted. The vessel moved back into the river.

At the same time, they heard a different, crunching sort of sound from the other side of the compound. The boys shuffled up the roof again to the ridgeline and peered over. The black truck had emerged from under the camouflage netting, headlamps beaming. It made its way across the compound and over to the inlet. It had huge wheels, a long wheel base and a ladder bolted to its side, rising to a roof-rack on the top. It made no sound as it travelled across the open area, rather like an expensive electric car would in our world. Four figures emerged from the truck and unloaded various crates into the plain-looking building, before one of them returned the truck to the car park and sauntered across the compound and into the guards' tower on the opposite side. Silence descended once more.

Jason slithered down from the roofline and slumped to the bottom, resting his head against the tiles. He closed his eyes. His head ached, his ankle ached, his nerves were shot. They had been here for over an hour now and, so far, found nothing. The closest they had come was the huge screen in the security office, but even then, they'd barely had time to look at it. A few more seconds ticked by, and his thoughts began to drift to Kia whilst the cold night breeze rustled his hair. Then he sat up straight. The screen.

Jason tugged at Joe's leg. "The screen."

"What about it?" His friend slid down beside him.

"That huge screen in the office," he waved his hands. "It was divided into seven sections."

"Yeah."

"One section was for the open area in the compound below us, right?"

"Right."

"And the remaining six we thought were probably for six different areas?"

Joe let out a frustrated puff of air.

"But we've only seen five areas," Jason beamed. If he could have stood up and jumped around, he would have.

And then Joe understood. His eyes lit up and he gripped Jason's arm.

"A *sixth area*."

There was a part of the compound they had not yet found. Suddenly, a course of action began to take shape in Joe's head. But elation quickly turned to deflation. If they moved off the roof, they were in danger of discovery. Judging by the throbbing pain, Jason's damaged ankle meant he certainly couldn't run. Even if, by some miracle, they found the sixth building, how could they eavesdrop? How likely was it they would overhear anything at all?

"I wish I could talk to Kia," Jason said, once again resting his head on the tiles.

"Yeah," Joe responded, misunderstanding Jason's meaning, rubbing the gold ring around his right ear. "I don't know why the implants stopped working."

There was a pause. Then Joe said, "Actually...maybe we can talk to her."

Jason looked at him. "What do you mean?"

"Well, we've got the bugs, haven't we?" Joe grinned. He was rummaging in the drysack, looking for the small metal tin.

"Yes!" Jason responded.

Joe found the tin and grabbed it.

"We won't be able to hear them, but at least they'll know we're okay." He removed one of the buttons, pressed the little switch down and stuck the button to the inside of his shirt. Now he was transmitting.

25

A New Mission

"Hey, Kia. We're doing okay."

Everyone in XSHC jumped in surprise. Kia stared at the three technicians working on sound.

"Joe, Jason?" Kia asked, leaning closer to the screen, her heart thumping.

"We can't hear you." The boys' voices crackled.

Joe continued, "But we thought if we turned one of these bugs on, you could at least hear us. Jason hurt himself trying to jump for the skylight. His ankle's a bit swollen and he's testing the effectiveness of the painkillers."

"I'm okay, I'm okay," Jason's voice followed. "We're safe for now, but when the moon comes out, or worse, when dawn comes, we'll be obvious to anyone on the river. We're going to try and figure out how to get down from the roof and get this mission done."

And that was it.

After her flood of relief subsided, Kia was surprised to hear the usually subdued technicians spring to life, tapping hard on their screens and keyboards.

"Kia." The tall blonde technician called her over, his eyes alight. "Our main stalling point was that we couldn't figure out how to signal them to turn on a transmitter without alerting everyone else in the vicinity. But now they have already turned on the fourth transmitter, that problem has gone away. We should be able to get this up and running in under two hours."

Kia felt a breath she didn't realise she'd been holding leave her, and the tension in her shoulders begin to ease. But she had no time to relax. A message pinged into her control desk. She looked up at her friends.

"Guys, Xci1 has asked for you to return to the Summer Palace."

The four friends looked at each other with raised eyebrows. They were already quite tired, and now Kia wanted them to go on a four-hour tram journey back down to Ruwark?

"Why?" Marcia asked, but Kia shrugged. She could barely think about anything other than Jason and Joe.

"Do you think you can be ready to leave within the hour?" Kia carried on. "Xci1 said he'll brief you on the details as you travel."

Seeing the look on Kia's face, Marcia moved to join her at her desk, giving her shoulder a squeeze.

"I'm sure they'll be okay," she said in a low voice. "They've done this sort of thing before."

At the unexpected affection, Kia felt tears well in her eyes. She nodded, took a big gulp of her water and sank back into her desk chair, her hand wandering to her stomach.

Trey interjected, "It's getting quite late. Let's take a forty-minute break, walk around, step outside for some fresh air. We have a long night ahead of us, and many of us are already tired."

Marcia concurred. "I agree. Kia, come with me. Apparently there's a sky garden on the castle roof." As Marcia took her arm, Kia gave one last look at the technicians before allowing herself to be steered from the room and down the corridor to the elevators. Perhaps just five minutes would be okay.

*

"I still don't know why I wasn't told about Xci1's real plan at the pageant," Kia said as they reached the rooftop and emerged into the cold evening beneath an almost new moon in a cloudless sky. In front of them was a softly lit garden, with a row of trees stretching across the roof to their right, some raised beds full of various plants, a huge pergola, some hanging seats, and a rather attractive water feature with water falling down the large rocks into a deep pool in which swam some brightly coloured koi carp. They settled into a wide, hanging swing seat beside the waterfall.

"I mean, what was he thinking?" She shook her head. "If that graphene mask hadn't worked, he'd be dead. And then where would we be?"

Marcia grinned. "If you had known, you would have locked him in XSHC. Trey knew that."

"I still think I should have been told," Kia pouted. How could she be expected to oversee XSHC if she wasn't party to a central fact of the plans? It wasn't reasonable, pragmatic. Marcia patted her arm with an apologetic smile.

Kia sighed. The real upset that had been lingering at the back of her mind washed over her again. She swallowed her tears and sank back into the cushions.

"I have plans, Marcia," she began after a long silence, her voice small. Marcia looked at her.

"So many plans. Exams, university and a law degree, a legal career...I can't ruin all that. I'm not even seventeen. I'm in no place to...I don't have the skills to..." The words faded and the tears fell.

Marcia put an arm around Kia and squeezed her shoulders. "You know I'll remain your friend whatever you do, right? I'm here for you whatever." There were some moments of silence before Kia could speak again.

"But you think I shouldn't go through with the appointment."

"Yes," she said it carefully. "That's right."

Kia's eyes welled. "But Jason, he...he wants me to ruin my future. He doesn't care about all my plans. He just..." Kia couldn't explain, and words wouldn't come out again. Kia knew Jason didn't agree with her, but did that mean he didn't love her? It felt like it. How could someone love her and disagree with her about the need to protect her future plans? Marcia disagreed too. She said she loved Kia, but did she truly? Kia's nausea surged, forcing her to think of what she had planned for the following day. And then of injured Jason in enemy territory. Everything swam round and round in her head, a giant, never-ending whirlpool. Tears fell for a while.

Marcia simply sat and hugged her friend, giving her the time she needed to cry, to express her pain. There were so many things she wanted to say, but she said none of them. She just stayed close and let Kia be.

They sat there, listening to the waterfall and watching the fish swim calmly around in the pool beneath it. They took in all the plants and trees and cool serenity of the surroundings, with the battlements to the castle highlighted by carefully disguised uplighters. It really was quite beautiful. The surroundings slowly brought calm to Kia, and she sighed involuntarily. They both knew it was time to leave, but they held back.

It was Kia who said finally, with one last sigh, "Come on, Marcia. We need to go...and thank you."

*

Twenty minutes later, Marcia, Trey, Max and Zika were seated in the tram on their way back to Ruwark Castle. Marcia flicked the communication switch, depressed the green button beside it and gave the call sign.

"Arelard X four two zero three," she said, "four en route and making for Ruwark."

"Ruwark X three zero two four," came the response. "One moment."

There was a brief pause, and then Xci1's strong voice came over the intercom.

"Friends, I ought to be doing one thing only: thanking you on behalf of the Anasiun people. It is only because of your resourcefulness and willingness to put yourselves in harm's way that we have the assassin in custody. But friends, we may have won the battle, but we have not won the war. There is more to be done. Kia is working tirelessly to oversee Jason and Joe's dangerous mission into Turonia as they gather evidence. But I am speaking to you now because we need your help again.

"First, we need to get the assassin to tell us what she knows. We need to persuade her that imparting the information will result in a far better future both for her and for the whole of the southern continent. Second, we need to use her as bait to entice Turonia to send a second assassin – an assassin we intend to apprehend as undeniable proof of their duplicity and aggression."

"Yes, Your Highness," Trey responded, as the others gave each other wide-eyed looks. Another assassin. Another trap.

"Max," Xci1 continued. "I need you at the Summer Palace to manage the technical side of our trap. Zika, you're the only person in all of Anasius trained by the highly secretive Underlord Academy with the unique skill set that such training provides. If we're going to catch this second assassin, I need you right here in Ruwark. Trey, you have demonstrated fearless loyalty to Anasius, so you can oversee the security personnel. And Marcia, I need you most of all."

"Me?" Marcia asked from her place in the driving seat.

"You're the only one who has any hope of success in talking to the assassin."

“I thought you just wanted me to drive the others…”

“She needs a young woman, someone not too much older than her. And I don’t think she’ll listen to anyone from Anasius. As far as she’s concerned, we’re the enemy.”

“Can’t you send someone else? I don’t have any experience with getting people to talk – that’s what interrogators are for.” Marcia’s mouth was dry.

“Marcia, you’re not from Anasius. You’re an outsider, like she is. She just needs to understand that there are good things in the world; there are good people who are not just out to exploit others. You need to make her see it.”

“But what if I can’t?”

“If there’s a chance she will talk, we have to try.” This time it was Trey who interjected. He had shuddered as Marcia mentioned the word interrogators. It reminded him of his horrific experience in Crask all those months ago. Interrogators were people who, through pain and suffering and misery, took everything from you. If the assassin would be given Marcia instead, it was a mercy.

Marcia bit her lip. She accepted the task with a nod.

“Excellent,” Xci1 said from the intercom. “Now for the rest of you.”

What followed was a detailed explanation of an audacious plan to capture a second Turonian assassin the following day. It was both cunning and dangerous. And if the assassin came out of it alive, Trey for one would be surprised.

26

Interrogation

Prisoners in Turonia were treated worse than animals. They were kept in individual cages in damp, cold dungeons, fed watery vegetable stew when the prison guards could be bothered, and not given access to even the most basic sanitation. Guards abused whichever prisoners they liked whenever they liked. Many prisoners died from that, hypothermia or starvation. No-one cared. They were prisoners getting what they deserved. And if a prisoner was unlucky enough to have some information useful to the Emperor, they were tortured until they revealed it or until they died.

Hera expected the same fate as she was transferred from the hospital to the dungeons of the Summer Palace in Ruwark. At first, she could not understand why Xci1 had not had her killed at the moment of her capture. But then she realised that the information she held was valuable to him. Information about Turonia, the Order of the Dragon, her training, the missions she had been on, and Turonia's ultimate intentions. She was not a traitor, but she assumed that unless she talked, the last few days of her life at the mercy of Anasius' best interrogators would be days of unimaginable pain. And whilst she kept her face wooden, secretly she was terrified.

Imagine her surprise, then, when she found herself locked in a cell not just with walls and bars, but also with a bed, a sink and a little desk and chair. Imagine her astonishment when she was brought food regularly, escorted to a presentable bathroom and given clean clothes and blankets to keep her warm. She was confused. Did they not want information from her? And then the moment had come when Xci1 himself had arrived and seated himself on the other side of the bars from her.

"I am Xci1, Prince of Anasius, Overlord to the Handed Isles and second only to Xcion the Sovereign who reigns over all things. And who might you be?"

Hera sat upright on her chair, resisting the temptation to say, "And I'm the Queen of Turonia and the biggest pain in the butt you've had for a long time." Instead, she kept it short.

"Hera."

"Hera? That is a regal name. It doesn't sound Turonian." Xci1 spoke it like a question.

"Well, it is," Hera lied.

Xci1's lips twitched. It could almost have been a smile.

"Before anything else, can you reassure me that you are being properly treated here?" he asked. "Are my officers treating you well?"

Hera was confused. This guy called himself a prince. A real prince would have watched eagerly as a prisoner such as herself was tortured and humiliated until they laid bare everything they knew. But this guy? "He doesn't deserve the title," she thought. "He's soft and useless."

"I have nothing to say," she said, pushing her shoulders back and glaring at him.

Xci1 took a deep breath. "Well, that's up to you. Someone else is coming to talk to you shortly. At noon tomorrow." He checked the time on his Scroll as he spoke and realised it was 1am. "Apologies, at noon *today*, we'll be transferring you to our facility in Ducal City. We'll make it known via our media channels in a few hours' time, hinting that you have offered to tell us everything provided we don't push for the death sentence for you. We have also invited Turonia to provide you with an attorney to help you navigate the trial and to look out for the interests of Turonia. Together, the news of a transfer and the invitation for an attorney should be enough to elicit a response from Turonia. If they decide to send an attorney, they are admitting that you are Turonian, which helps us. If they refuse, then most likely they'll be scrambling to get someone here for noon today to try and deal with you before you can talk. That gives us an opportunity to capture another Turonian. Good plan, right?"

Hera swallowed, trying hard to keep her face expressionless. "They won't send an attorney. And if they send an assassin for me, you'll have succeeded in getting me killed, and end up with another silent assassin in my place."

Xci1 looked into her pale green eyes and knew a wave of sadness. What had happened in such a short life to produce such an icy, impenetrable heart? He shook his head. He hoped Marcia would have more success with her than he did.

"Why don't you get a few hours of sleep? The rest of today is going to be busy." He left her in the dungeons and ascended the stairs back into the Summer Palace itself. He returned to the command centre in the dressing room beside the ballroom. The security team went over their plans once again.

*

Four hours later, Marcia pulled the tram up to the platform beneath the Summer Palace. Max, Trey and Zika had somehow managed to get some fitful sleep in the tram, each of them lying across four of the seats and nodding off to the quiet rhythm of the wheels on the almost impossibly smooth paved ground. As the tram slowed, the rhythm changed, and they stirred. Trey rubbed the tiredness out of his eyes and sat up as the tram came to a complete halt. He checked the time. 3am. Thoughts of the last couple of days rushed in on him. The extraction. The pageant. The assassin.

"I'm not sure I'm going to be able to get that assassin to talk." Marcia broke the silence, turning to face them but keeping her eyes fixed on the floor. She had been dwelling on the task in front of her for the past four hours and a pit of dread had begun to pool in her stomach. "I'm really not the one for this job." She crossed her arms.

Max shook himself, stood up and stamped his feet. "You'll do great," he said. "Just be yourself. Tell her about yourself. Don't try and draw her out, she'll feel manipulated. Just share yourself and try to get to know her a bit. Try and befriend her. I don't reckon she'll be expecting that."

Marcia jumped down from the cab onto the platform and the four friends walked up the stairs to the entrance hall at the Summer Palace.

"Yeah, you'll be fine," Trey agreed. "At least you haven't got to meet a bunch of senior security personnel and try and pretend you know what you're doing even though they're all double your age. You've just got to have a chat with someone younger than you."

Marcia hadn't thought about it that way. "You guys will be fine too. Look how you managed to capture the assassin in the first place."

"I did nothing of the sort," Zika said. "I just sat up a bunch of scaffolding for eight hours, trying to locate her through a pair of binoculars. And failing."

"And all I did was persuade the actor and make sure he looked perfect before I let him leave. And the actor only ended up being a decoy anyway," Max lamented.

Trey suddenly spoke up, "Turonia aren't going to want to put another assassin in harm's way, are they? So they'll probably get the second assassin to take our assassin out from a distance. And the only obvious place to do that is—"

"—Ruwark's Needle," Max finished.

"Or the city wall," Zika suggested.

"That's miles away," Marcia protested, recalling Ruwark's geography. "No-one could take a shot from there."

"Yeah," Trey agreed. "Unlikely."

"No," Zika returned. "What about along the eastern edge of the city? It gets much closer to the palace."

"True..." Trey shrugged. Max and Marcia looked unconvinced.

The friends arrived in the entrance hall at this point and were greeted by Xci1. He led them to the dressing room where the command centre was abuzz. Leaving Trey and Zika there to go over their plans, he escorted Max and Marcia to the top of the stairs leading down to the dungeons, but then he invited Marcia to continue on down by herself.

"All we've gleaned from her so far is that her name is Hera," Xci1 said. "And don't worry, she's in a cell so she cannot hurt you. Just stay a good distance away from the bars to avoid trouble. Max will listen in to the conversation. May Xcion the Sovereign oversee you and bring you success." With that, Xci1 returned to the situation room and left Max and Marcia alone.

Marcia's palms began to sweat.

"She won't want to talk to me." Marcia spoke aloud the worry that had not stopped whirling around her mind.

Max shrugged. "You have to try." Then, seeing her face, he added, "All you can do is be yourself. No-one can ask for more than that."

And so Marcia found herself descending the stairs to the dungeons. Her heartbeat grew faster with each step and her throat began to close up. "Be yourself," she muttered, recalling Max's words. She took a deep breath.

*

Hera stirred at the sound of her name.

"Hera," the voice repeated. "I'm sorry to wake you."

Hera groaned and kept her eyes firmly closed. The truth was that she had not really been able to sleep, despite feeling exhausted. Her stomach was churning, and she was confident she was into the last twenty-four hours of her short life.

"I'm so sorry," the voice continued. "And I know it's a crazy time of night, but I need to chat to you."

Hera groaned again and gave in.

"What time is it?" she asked, sitting up. She saw, standing close to the bars, a black girl with deep brown eyes, of above average height and in Anasiun dress. Hera froze for a moment, gathering her sensibilities like one of the deer she used to target in training.

"My name's Marcia, and it's very early," Marcia admitted. "To be honest, I'd rather be asleep, too. But we need to talk." The girl, Marcia, moved to sit on a chair and looked through the bars of the cell as Hera stared at her.

"Marcia," Hera repeated, not taking her eyes off the unfamiliar figure.

"Sorry, I'm doing this badly. I just...drive trams, to be honest." Marcia flushed. Why had she said that?

"A girl who drives trams?" Hera mocked with cold eyes, before asking, "What kind of a job is that?"

Marcia blushed. She had often thought the same thing. Her friends took all these brave risks, and all she ever did was drive them around...in trams. No-one ever said it, but she knew they thought it was pretty lame.

“I know.” She looked at her feet. “I kind of wonder why I’m part of all this stuff.”

Hera raised an eyebrow. Usually, Marcia's kind of remark would be met with animosity. Maybe a punch.

“The thing is,” Marcia continued, “I’m not actually from Anasius so I don’t really need a job here at all. I don’t come here often.” Marcia had no idea how to explain the whole “being extracted” and coming from a different world thing. Hera would think she was insane.

Hera said nothing.

“It’s hard to explain,” Marcia carried on into the silence. “I guess the shorthand version is that whilst I am not Anasiun, I know Anasius quite well. I have a great respect for the country and way it is governed. And I’ve been involved in …” she stopped, unsure how to explain. “Anasius is a country which places high value on respect, courage, honesty, integrity, diligence and freedom,” she started again. “Where I come from, whilst people talk of such values, many of those who govern do not actually live by them. Here, it’s different. Anasius’ governance is built upon those principles. It seeks to nurture its citizens and respect its neighbours, to defend its borders and uphold the law. I think Turonia is different though, right?”

Unable to keep the contempt from her face any longer, Hera couldn’t help but speak.

“Honesty? Integrity? Those are weak character traits for those who can’t stomach the real world.” She spat on the floor near Marcia’s feet. “Where I come from, we applaud the strong and the brave and the powerful and the wealthy.

To govern a country, you cannot be weak, you have to be ruthless, and you fight for power and control and money."

Shocked by such sudden aggression from such a young girl, Marcia was cowed by Hera's tone of voice almost as much as the words she spoke.

"But for the leaders of a country, isn't that a bit self-centred? It doesn't sound like the attitude you would need from someone who should be interested in freedom."

Hera scoffed again.

"Freedom! You speak as if freedom could provide anything other than anarchy. If everyone were free, anyone could do anything. You'd have no rule of law, no control of the people, no ability to grow your country in wealth, power and influence on the international stage. It's hardly surprising Anasius is so small and insignificant."

"Anasius isn't insignificant. Anasius successfully repelled an attempted invasion by Notalia in 316. Anasius overthrew a despotic, power-hungry leader and returned a team of Elders to its rightful royal rule governing. And Anasius has now been ruled successfully with integrity and freedom for over 500 years. Turonia has existed for less than half that time. That speaks for itself."

Hera paused.

"How did a country that values respect and freedom ever manage to win a war?" she found herself asking.

Marcia dragged her chair nearer the bars of the cell.

"I'll tell you the story," she said. And then she outlined what had happened at the Notalian Invasion of 316, being careful to omit her own part in the story. As she detailed the events, Hera's shoulder's relaxed as she got drawn into the drama of Marcia's words. All her life, Hera had been told that Anasius was a small, irrelevant, cowardly country. But as Marcia's words described the events of the past, Hera felt the image of it in her mind start to crack.

"It's good we've taken Notalia then," she blurted out, on the offensive. "After your war with Notalia, Anasius simply let them return to live within their borders once more. But we've taken over and now they're under Turonian command. And we didn't fight any war at all."

"Oh?" Marcia's heart began to race at Hera's unashamed admission of Turonia's damming work. It was exactly the evidence they had been looking for. She hoped Max was paying attention behind the wall.

"It only took six or seven people to die for us to take Notalia. And we improved their infrastructure whilst we were at it. How many people died in *your* war?"

"The war we fought was to defend our country from outside aggression," Marcia pushed back. "It was honourable. I'm not sure how honourable it is to assassinate those who won't give in and pay off those who do just to subjugate a whole nation without them ever realising it. And what good is infrastructure that lulls people into servitude and lines the pockets of traitors in power? It seems disingenuous, deceitful and dishonourable to me."

These words stung Hera. Her whole life was built on the idea of honour. Honour gained through diligence and painful endurance and determination. Honour demanded from those in power, and willingly given by all those below them. Fighters honoured for their ability to win, to hurt, to maim, to kill; honoured for their willingness to do what was necessary for the good of the country, no questions asked. Marcia's words spoke of a different kind of honour, an honour that sounded...higher? Hera's mind was a whirlpool.

Marcia took a change of direction. "I know everyone says you're Turonian, and maybe you are, and I know that you will want to be loyal to your home country. For us here, though, this is not just about Anasius. This is about the whole of the southern continent trying to defend itself against an insidious enemy who is seeking to overthrow us all by stealth. In a couple of hours, all the countries of the southern continent will know of Turonia's ambitions. And if Turonia cannot bring itself to withdraw, we will go to war. We have fought tyrants before, and we will do it again. And this time, Turonia will be fighting out in the open, in real, honest, battle, against all the countries of the southern continent. It has no hope of winning that fight."

Hera grinned at her. "For starters, you have no proof," she said. "They'll just deny your story. No-one's going to take you seriously—"

"—This very conversation is proof. You yourself have confirmed that Turonia have toppled Notalia. The message to the southern continent can now be brought with words from your own mouth."

Hera opened her mouth to respond, but no sound came out. The horror of it hit her like a tornado. All of a sudden, she realised she had been goaded to speak. And now her words were her own undoing. Her face flushed; her stomach dropped. What had she done? The Emperor would learn of her words and he would ensure her end. She had no doubt.

Marcia saw the colour drain from Hera's usually proud face. She saw her shoulders sink. She felt a sudden pang of pity for the girl, realising for the first time that, lethal assassin though she was, she was only young.

"Hera, you *say* you are Turonian. But your skin, your name...I am not convinced, I think..."

"It doesn't matter what you think," Hera broke in. Her eyes were bleak. "Do you know what you've done? As soon as the Emperor hears of my failure, of my words, he will deny everything and ensure I die. He will be furious. And no-one, no person, no city and certainly no country wants to make the Emperor furious. He has people working for him in many countries and in high places. His reach is huge. He is merciless and mighty; nothing can stand in his way. Don't you see? When that message goes out, you'll have poked a sleeping dragon." Somehow, despite the wave of defeat, Hera was still combative. It was not in her nature to surrender.

"Well, even if you are from Turonia, what do you have to gain from being loyal to them? You'll die."

"To go against Turonia would be treason. It would be to dishonour myself and the country. And I am a woman of honour," Hera's eyes flashed.

"If Turonia is not your country, then you can't commit treason in it," Marcia countered, her logic inescapable. "Only a citizen of a country can commit treason. And it seems to me that to fail to bring Turonia to justice is dishonouring. What about your family? What will they think?"

"They already think I'm dead."

"And dishonouring them doesn't matter?" Marcia's reply was brutal, but perhaps Hera responded better to harshness.

In Hera's mind's eye, she could see the night she was kidnapped and taken to Turonia. Her chest tensed as she felt the horror of it, the aching void created by the sudden loss of her family. She realised that she had built a wall around her heart to protect it, but that behind that wall, in the core of her being, she still ached for her family, for love. She was a highly tuned fighter and assassin who already had eight marks on her kill sheet, each one adding a layer of cement to that wall. But now, in the space of a short conversation, a brick or two had been knocked loose. "Disingenuous, dishonourable and deceitful." Marcia's words, Xcil's sadness, the warmth of Mark and Layla's home...it all echoed around her head. Why was she loyal to the Emperor? What had he ever done for her? In that moment she realised, with sudden, sickening clarity, that all the accolades and encouragements and promises of future wealth and fame that had been proclaimed during her Black Ops training were probably empty. Those promises were not because the Emperor cared about her, but because he wanted to use her. She was a pawn in his egotistical ambition. It was as if scales had fallen from her eyes. For the first time, she could see.

Sitting on the bed, a mixture of exhaustion and regret washed over her, and she withdrew into herself. She only had a few hours left to live and there was nothing more to say. Marcia realised she was going to get no further.

"At noon today you're being moved from here to a secure location in Tsarn. I hope you survive the transport." And with that, and a clang as the gate rattled shut, Marcia left the dungeons.

Hera was left alone with her thoughts and one new, unfamiliar companion: despair.

27

Breaking in

Jason and Joe decided they had no time to rest. Jason, realising how dry his mouth was, found his water bottle from one of the dry bags and had a few swigs. Joe followed suit.

"Let's find this sixth area," he whispered.

Jason wriggled his foot and found it not nearly as painful as he thought it would be. The tight bandage was helping.

"There might be a way down at the far end," he said, pointing towards the southern edge of the building.

The two boys closed the drybags and crawled their way across the roof to the far end. It seemed to take forever, but they made it and peered carefully over the edge into the space between them and the southern wall of the compound. They could make out a few trees and park benches dotted about, some plants and flowers in raised beds, and a little pool in the middle. But there was no clear way of getting down from the roof except for an alarmingly big jump. It would be impossible for Jason.

Jason shook his head. He knew Joe would be prepared to risk it, but he'd already been foolish once today. After a chat, they began the long shuffle back across the entire roof to the far end by the car park. As they progressed, the moon came out from behind a cloud and bathed the area in a soft light once again. Thankfully there were no boats on the river.

At the northern end of the roof, they had more luck. The camouflage netting stretched out from the building, perhaps two metres below the ridgeline in the centre, but only half a metre below the roof at its lowest points. The netting stretched out mostly flat, but then rose up to meet the plain building on the north side of the compound, providing complete covering for the corner and the north side before the plain building. It was easy to see that even Jason could position himself over the side of the roof and get his feet onto the netting without much difficulty. What they did not know was whether the netting would take their weight. There was only one way to find out.

The boys decided that Joe should go first, since he would have more chance of escape if the netting broke. Joe swung his legs over the side of the building. He got a purchase with his feet and then, gripping onto the roof with his hands, he eased his weight from the rooftop to the netting. The netting made no complaint, and whilst it did shake somewhat with Joe's weight, it looked like it was going to be okay. Joe took the drybags from Jason and made his way to the centre of the netting, staying well away from the front edge and the open area of the compound below it. He moved spread-eagled, trying to disperse his weight as much as possible, and peering through the netting at the car park below. As he was crawling above the truck they had seen earlier, he had an idea. He removed the knife from his belt hook and began to cut the straps of the netting. After three or four cuts, he was able to push the strapping apart to make a decent-sized hole. Clutching the drybags, he dropped through onto the roof rack of the truck, just a few feet below him, landing like a cat. It was deathly quiet in the compound.

As soon as Joe had dropped from the netting, Jason started his own journey across. He reached the hole and looked through the netting. Joe was sitting cross-legged on the top of the truck.

"If you stick your legs through and lower yourself like you did from the roof, it should be pretty easy," he whispered.

Joe was right. He would not need to jump onto his injured foot at all. He swung around, gripped onto the netting with both hands and lowered himself down. After they were both sitting on the truck with their bags, ready to plan their next move, Joe pushed the straps of the netting back together, disguising the hole he had made.

They peered out into open space and began assessing the area. Where was the Black Ops training ground? The entrance had to be somewhere in the compound.

"What about the far side of that hut?" Jason pointed to the place where the car park met the plain building. "There could be something on the other side? We could stick to the shadows and have a look."

Joe agreed. As they whispered, they became aware of a familiar noise. Another boat was approaching from the river. They froze. What if, once again, the very truck upon which they sat was about to be used to take cargo around the compound? They needed to move.

Joe grabbed the bags and crawled along the ladder on the roof and down to the compound floor, closely followed by Jason. He winced as his weight fell on his left foot. But, to his relief, it was bearable. As soon as they began their descent on the truck ladder, they were visible in the half-light of the moon. Anyone looking in their direction would see them without difficulty. They needed to hide, and fast.

Reaching the hardened dirt floor, they rushed across to the back of the netting, which was in deeper shadow, casting about for a decent hiding place. But as their eyes scanned the car park, there was nowhere obvious to hide at all. Apart from the truck and a couple of much smaller vehicles, the rest was an open space interrupted only by a few bollards and the occasional plant or small tree. The car park was bordered by the high, razor-wire-topped walls. The front of the car park was open. There was a row of tall metal pillars running across the front edge, keeping the netting in place, but they were too narrow to be a hiding place.

"Quick," Jason whispered. "Under the truck!" It was the only option. The boys raced back to the truck, hit the floor and slithered underneath, dragging the drybags after them. They held their breath, their hearts pounding, waiting for a shout from the open compound from someone who had seen their descent from the roof, their hasty run to the deeper shadows, or their faster dash back to the comparative safety of the truck. But no shout came. They had not been seen.

As they began to breathe again, they rolled over and stared up at the underside of the truck, which offered, for the most part, a smooth undercarriage from the tailgate all the way to behind the front wheels. However, between the cab floor and the truck itself was a gap that extended most of the width and rose perhaps half-a-metre upwards before meeting the top of the wheel arches. It looked like it could be large enough to accommodate them. Joe pointed at it.

"Worth a try?" He shuffled towards it and reached up into the darkness to try and find a handhold. His hands closed around what felt like a piece of angle iron and he hauled himself upwards, willing his eyes to adjust to the darkness. Moments later he began to pick out the edges of the niche and the steel struts which held the chassis together. He pulled himself up fully into the space, hooking his knees over the lower strut and gripping onto the slightly higher one with his hands. It was not comfortable, and he couldn't sustain the position for long, but it would work for the moment.

"Hand me the bags," he whispered. Then he hauled them up and pushed them behind his head into the smaller gap above the wheel arch.

The discovery of the niche wasn't a moment too soon. Tramping across the compound towards the car park from the guard tower, they could see a pair of shiny black boots and the hem of a black cape. Someone was coming.

"Come on, Jas," Joe urged him in a fierce whisper. But Jason was already moving. It took him slightly longer to get in place than Joe, but within a few seconds, Jason was ensconced next to him, wondering what would happen next.

Black Boots opened the cab door and climbed up into the truck. Moments later, it began to move almost silently again, save for the wheels making a soft "crunch" on the hardened earth. Jason and Joe clung on, praying there would be no potholes. The truck sped up, crossed the compound in under two minutes and then slowed to a stop just to the east of the river inlet, under the camouflage netting which, again, was kept aloft by the same tall, thin metal pillars.

Now they could hear a number of voices: men having quiet, overlapping conversations. There was much scuffling and grunting and hushed complaining as a second set of crates was loaded onto the truck ready to be distributed around the compound. The boys under the truck were trying to work out how many men there were, but it was too confusing to make out, and their arms were beginning to ache.

Six sets of dusty boots and the hems of their capes could be seen in a neat row just off to the left of the truck. Then a seventh set of polished black boots could be seen facing the six, along with the unmistakable gold-trimmed boots of Turonian royalty.

"Good evening, Your Highness," came a shaky, mid-range male voice, followed by several quieter voices.

"Your Highness."

"Your Highness."

The first voice came again, "We were not expecting you this evening, Your Highness, or we would have arranged for a car to transport you. I hesitate to ask, but would you be prepared to ride in the truck?"

Then came a much deeper, gravelly voice. "General, if I had wanted to ride in my car, I would have informed you I was coming. I am here to give Operation Goldensun to one of your youngest and best officers. I will meet with him, and you are to organise his mission field kit according to these instructions." To the boys it sounded like the General was handing over a piece of paper. "Have everything ready to go within the hour," the Royal continued. Jason and Joe looked at each other.

"Of course, Your Highness," said Black Boots. "Our officers are always ready to serve Turonia. But which officer...?"

"Read the instructions," Royal Boots interrupted him. "And, in answer to your first question, no."

"Sir?"

"I will not ride in the truck. I am going to drive it."

With that, he climbed into the carriage and the truck began to reverse so fast that Jason almost lost his grip. Joe grabbed his shirt.

"Always happy to save your skin," he whispered over the roar of the engine with a grin.

Jason opened his mouth to argue, but then he let it go. Perhaps Joe had a point.

The truck stopped and lurched forwards, accelerating across the compound away from the inlet and towards the guard tower. They had to hold on tight as the truck moved across the compound, their hands and knees burning in pain. It took two minutes before it slowed down and came to a halt.

Hanging beneath the truck, it was impossible to see where they were going, but for any uninitiated observer on the outside, what happened next would have been stupefying. The truck stopped at the keypad and retinal scanner by the eastern gate, next to the guard tower. The driver leaned out, punched an eight-digit code into the keypad, and turned his head and stared into the retinal scanner. Moments later, the truck lights were extinguished along with the light under the entranceway, leaving the truck in darkness. For a brief moment, it was hard to see what was happening, but when the entranceway light came on again twenty seconds later, the truck had vanished.

Under the truck, Jason and Joe had a very different experience. When the lights went out, by the soft moonlight they could still make out most of the building and inlet at the opposite end of the compound. Then, accompanied by a slight whining noise, the truck sank rapidly downwards, as if the ground had been removed from beneath it. The sudden movement took Joe and Jason completely by surprise and Joe banged his head on the chassis of the truck.

"Ow," he whispered, wanting to rub his head but unable to do so without falling from where he was hanging. Both boys by now were very uncomfortable indeed, and holding on was becoming increasingly difficult.

The truck stopped descending with a bump and then it rolled forwards off the red-brown dirt, down a shallow ramp and onto a dark flagstone floor. As it reached the flagstones, the rectangle of dirt behind them disappeared back upwards and out of view, pushed up by a large concertina-like structure in dark grey steel. They were clearly underground.

And suddenly the boys understood. The keypad and retinal scan were not to prevent people leaving the compound without authorisation. No, they were the necessary security to provide access to an underground bunker. This had to be the Black Ops training ground. The sixth area on the cameras in the security office. "By sheer good luck," as Joe put it later, they had gained entry to the hidden and secure underground bunker.

The boys were struggling. The lower strut was digging into the backs of their knees, their arms and shoulders ached, and they were finding it painful being folded almost in half in the cramped space by the wheel arch. The door to the truck opened and the royal figure strode away from the truck, his gold-trimmed black cape billowing out behind him. A second pair of black boots followed swiftly after him.

"Your Royal Highness, may I help?" he asked. But as both pairs of boots receded from the truck, it became impossible to hear what they were saying.

Finally, the boys pulled their legs over the bottom strut and lowered themselves onto the flagstones below, trying to stay hidden behind the huge wheels at the front of the truck. Joe reached up and pulled their dry bags out of the hole before he, too, rested a moment on the flagstones. The relief to their arms and shoulders and knees was instant, despite the hardness and coldness of the floor. Royal Boots had disappeared somewhere down a tunnel off to the left, with the second man following him. The boys peered out into the bunker, hunting about for somewhere to hide next.

By the light of the downlighters recessed into the roof, it was obvious that the bunker they were in was more like a large, concrete-lined hemisphere. Into the walls of the hemisphere were regularly spaced tunnels stretching away. Black Boots had entered the one which led to a dormitory area. Sticking out into the hemisphere just to the left beyond the truck was an empty security booth, usually manned by a single Black Ops officer. There didn't seem to be anyone around though they could still hear a murmur of voices from Royal Boots and the man who had followed him.

"Operation Goldensun," Joe whispered, repeating the overheard conversation. What do you think that's about?"

"I don't know."

"Maybe it's a second assassin," Joe shrugged.

"We need to find out." Jason opened one of the drybags, grabbed the tin of listening devices and removed the lid. "Look for somewhere to hide, Joe, and quickly," he instructed.

With no other warning, Jason was up and limp-running to the security office before Joe realised his intent. There was nothing he could do to help. Before finding a hiding place though, Joe searched out the security cameras. He spotted one at the roof of the security booth, pointing at the steel concertina. He guessed it was there to keep track of those who entered and left the bunker. He could see another one on the opposite side, pointing towards the tunnel the two men had disappeared down. A third was attached to the wall on their right, directed down the tunnel nearest to them. There didn't appear to be any others, which was fortunate for Jason who had now disappeared inside the security office.

He emerged a moment later and headed back towards Joe, limping and asking with his eyes and hands where they should hide. Joe pointed at the cameras. Jason's eyes widened as he realised how lucky he had been.

"There's nowhere to hide here," Joe whispered. "Everywhere is open. We need to try one of those two tunnels with no cameras."

Joe grabbed the bags and followed Jason into the tunnel. They did not have to go far before they realised they had entered a toilet and shower block. The toilets were all individual cubicles with sinks and mirrors opposite. Beyond them was a cleaning area with cloths, yellow cones and a mop and bucket. Then beyond that were the shower cubicles, each with its own pegs and bench outside, a drying area and then the cubicle and shower itself. But beyond the shower cubicles was a blank wall. It was a dead end. They retraced their steps.

Back in the hemisphere, they moved to the only other tunnel without a camera. This time the tunnel was a little longer, turned to the left and then broadened out into a cafeteria with kitchens off to the left. The cafeteria itself contained numerous tables, each one served by four metal high-backed chairs, a long counter with trays and cutlery and so on, and some glass-fronted cabinets. In the tunnel before the cafeteria was a line of numbered hooks, from one of which hung a black cape. Whilst there were plenty of places to shelter here, once the cafeteria was full, nowhere would be safe. They rushed back down the tunnel, now desperate to find somewhere to hide.

As they arrived back in the hemisphere, they could hear voices coming down the first tunnel. They looked at each other in panic. What to do? Joe grabbed Jason's arm and pulled him towards the shower block.

"Quick," he said.

Joe propelled Jason into the last toilet cubicle and then grabbed a yellow cone from just beyond it. Understanding, Jason entered the cubicle and climbed onto a little shelf above the toilet, his feet resting on the cistern. Joe put the yellow cone quickly on the floor outside and then pulled it and the door closed behind them both. He locked the door and bent down to squint through the crack. Hopefully, for anyone who entered the toilet block, the furthest toilet's cubicle with its locked door and yellow cone outside would be enough to suggest the toilet was out of use.

Joe's actions came not a moment too soon. He could make out a small group of people coming down the tunnel towards them, making light conversation. They looked dishevelled, lots of them carrying their capes and keycards.

"...never expected His Highness to arrive in our dormitory."

"What were we supposed to do? You can't bow if you're lying in bed."

"Think about Raynor," one voice laughed. "He's rubbish at getting up at the best of times. I'm surprised he didn't just roll over and go back to sleep." Laughter rang around the room.

"I'm surprised he's still on the programme."

"Shut up," was the response. "My skills are far better than yours. He won't want to lose me just because of a bit of sleep." To Jason and Joe, Raynor sounded like he was trying to convince himself as much as his comrades.

"Hurry up," someone else said. "He's only given us five minutes and we need showers." A few people used the toilets, but thankfully no-one tried their cubicle and they remained hidden. A minute or so later, all they could hear was showers running.

A dangerous thought leapt into Joe's brain. Despite Jason's silent protestation, he silently unlocked the door, pushed the cone out of the way and tiptoed rapidly across to the shower cubicles, keeping a sharp eye out as he went. At the first cubicle, he found what he was looking for. Clothing, a towel and a cape. He took what he needed and returned swiftly to the toilet cubicle, where Jason was peering out. Joe held up his hand. He also had grabbed a keycard.

"This may come in handy," he whispered with a grin. Jason had no time to respond, because no sooner had Joe pulled the cone across and shut the door, someone opened their shower cubicle.

"Hurry up guys, we've got less than a minute left!"

What followed was a flurry of activity. Shower doors banged. Towels flew through the air. Clothes were pulled on, boots were laced up, capes were donned and the four or five people who'd come into the tunnel raced back towards the hemisphere, leaving a detritus of wet towels, dripping showers, dropped bottles and little rivulets of water. The tunnel fell silent.

Jason and Joe emerged from the cubicle, surveying the scene before them. Jason had the presence of mind to refill their water bottles. They tiptoed back down the tunnel towards the hemisphere, and, to their horror, realised that the security booth was no longer empty. An officer was sitting in it, his feet up on a desk, staring at a screen off to the left of the window. Even if he didn't look in their direction, he would surely notice movement to his left as they emerged from the tunnel. There was no way for them to leave. They were stuck.

28

XSHC in Action

Kia was overwhelmed. They were beginning to receive intel from the listening devices Jason and Joe had planted, but it was impossible to decipher anything meaningful from the conversations streaming into XSHC security personnel earphones.

"Time to talk to the new recruits...not again...who is the best fighter?...look at the...golden sun..."

"It's all useless." Kia threw down her headphones and pressed her fingers to her temples. "There's too much to listen to at once. And as far as I can make out, they're just posturing or complaining about their training or the weather."

"We need more ears on this," the lead technician agreed, signalling to two others to take a seat. He glanced at Kia. The atmosphere in the room was tense. No-one dared mention Joe, and especially Jason.

Despite the technician's promises, communications still hadn't been restored and the satellite view of the Order of the Dragon compound hadn't revealed a hopeful picture.

As soon as they saw Joe start his crawl seemingly across the treetops, Kia commanded that the satellite picture be magnified and enhanced as much as possible. They had realised he was crawling across a camouflage net. Then they had watched as the boys disappeared from view and a truck appeared, driving across the compound to the gate at the eastern wall. They fully expected it to pass under the wall and out onto the road, but again it disappeared. The analysts studied the footage up and down the roadway, but there was no sign of the truck, and having studied the tyre tracks both before and after the lights were extinguished, one analyst was adamant that it had not left the compound.

"It couldn't have gone underground, could it?" A younger analyst had suggested. There was a silence as everyone digested the idea. An underground area would explain the truck's disappearance and why the training ground couldn't be seen via satellite. Were the boys there too?

Wherever they were, Jason and Joe must have been hard at work as the XSHC office had soon filled with the "pings" of transmissions from more listening devices. Kia just wished she could speak to them.

*

Hera turned over on the bed and, in so doing, woke up. It took her a moment to remember where she was, but when she did, all the events of the past day crowded in on her mind. Why had her shot not killed Xci1? How had she allowed herself to be caught? That girl Marcia had threatened to send a message to the southern continent – had it gone out to the world by now? Was there, even now, a ruthless assassin preparing to take her down as she left Ruwark Castle at noon? And what about Turonia? The thought of her home country made her stomach turn cold. What should she be feeling about that? Within moments, her mind was in a whirl. She got up and paced back and forth, trying to sort out her thinking.

Only a few minutes after Marcia had left her, Hera had been visited once more – this time by three security officers, an older man and a teenage boy – both of them looking nervous. They had led her, handcuffed, to a strange contraption and told her to put her head in it. With some resistance, she had obeyed. The boy – Max he'd said his name was – had explained what was going on whilst the man had pushed some buttons and a metal arm had spun 360 degrees around her head, flashing orange. Hera didn't know if she believed that they were just taking pictures, or if they'd somehow implanted something in her. It didn't matter to her anyway; she wasn't going to live much longer.

What Hera hadn't known was that her images had flown to the Director of a small business in Juntaou's capital city. That very minute, at 3am, the Director had sent the attached file to his 3D printing system and ended up with an accurate replica of Hera's head that he began to mould. At 4:12am, the nineteen-year-old son from a second business had taken the mask into another building a few blocks away and fitted it with graphene. The entire process look less than thirty minutes. At 4:58am, the mask was handed to a speedboat owner who placed the package carefully on the bottom of the boat, securing it with bungees. Then the speedboat headed downriver towards Arelard, a journey that, at his speed, took less than two hours. By 7:25am, it was on a tram on its way to the Summer Palace at Ruwark so it could be fitted to Hera's face. Never before had a graphene mask been ordered, engineered, produced and delivered in under nine hours.

"I'm glad you're awake."

Hera turned around. It was Marcia's voice, and she was accompanied by Max.

"I'll call up for breakfast, you must be starving," Max said.

Hera's confusion was back. Surely a prisoner should only be fed if absolutely necessary? And she'd be dead soon anyway. Why eat?

"I thought I was being transferred at noon?" she asked.

"You are. But you'll need to get your strength up. And when they bring your food down, they'll take you to the bathroom as well. Do you want a shower?"

Hera's confusion grew further. "Didn't you listen last night? Turonia are going to kill me. What's the point of showering?"

Max grinned at her. "No, no. Turonia are going to *try* to kill you. But they won't succeed. Not if we have anything to do with it."

Two guards were coming down the corridor, one carrying a tray of food. Hera couldn't get her brain around what was going on. She couldn't even formulate a question.

So she just nodded and let a guard take her across to the bathrooms and showers.

Fifteen minutes later, Hera was finishing off a very delicious breakfast.

"You know, if they treated prisoners like this in Turonia, everyone would commit crimes."

Max laughed. "This is not standard prison food. I had something very similar myself an hour ago and asked for them to do the same for you."

"Why?"

"I dunno really," Max shrugged. "I guess I thought you would enjoy it."

"Hera, we need to talk to you about our plan," Marcia intervened, settling on a chair in front of her. "You know you took a potshot at Xci1 yesterday, here at the Summer Palace?"

Hera frowned. To demean her assassination attempt as "taking a potshot" was rather insulting.

"I got him square on the forehead," she said. "I just don't understand how anyone could survive that."

Marcia smiled. "The same way you're going to. We think Turonia will send an assassin who will try and take you out from a distance."

Hera nodded. She had come to the same conclusion before she had fallen asleep.

"Yes, it's the cleanest way to do it. The assassin would want to avoid anything close and personal. A shot from a distance would be the go-to move in a situation like this."

"How far away will the marksman shoot from?" Marcia asked.

Hera thought for a moment.

"We're mostly trained to shoot from up to 700m away. But we do have one or two fighters who could make the shot from up to a kilometre away if they needed to."

Max and Marcia looked at each other. That confirmed their two options: Ruwark's Needle or the eastern wall. But which one? Where should they send Zika to patrol?

"If you fail, I die," Hera said bluntly.

"No." Max shook his head. He explained about the body armour and the specially constructed graphene mask.

"So I didn't miss," Hera exclaimed, her food forgotten. "The mask stopped the bullet." She felt strangely vindicated. One mystery solved.

"Yes," Max said. "And it will stop the bullet meant for you too."

And suddenly, Hera understood. The Anasiuns were trying to engineer the capture of a second assassin from Turonia. Someone who could corroborate her story, a story which would make it very difficult for Turonia to explain away. She had to admit, it was ingenious.

"So...I might not die today?" Hera was tentative.

"No," Marcia said. "In fact, I'd put money on it."

"But surely you'll execute me at some point anyway? I mean, I've killed some people. So even if you give me a fair trial, murder is a capital offence in any country, isn't it?"

Marcia was tempted to argue. After all, there is now no such thing as a capital offence back in England. But instead, she said, "In Anasius, first-degree murder is a capital offence, yes. But some mitigating circumstances commute that capital verdict to a prison sentence of some kind. And someone under eighteen cannot be tried for murder. Anyway, in your case you were following orders. It could be argued that the Turonian high command are more culpable than you are."

Hera was not convinced at all, but she didn't argue. Instead, she asked, "What if I don't cooperate?"

"What d'you mean?" Marcia asked, confused.

"What if I have to be carried kicking and screaming to the transport vehicle?"

"Then I expect the security officers will pull your mask off and leave you to the assassin," Max said. "But I don't know why you would. You have an opportunity here. An opportunity to bring some honour back to your family. An opportunity not just to kill off a few unsuspecting random strangers, but to unseat a tyrannical emperor. You could be instrumental in bringing down the country that has treated you as an asset – a piece of military hardware to be discarded without a thought if it goes wrong. You could allow yourself to be a human being again. Whilst you may be a convicted killer, you could also be a hero who saves the southern continent. And that has *got* to be something in your favour in the courts."

Hera was silent. Since her conversation with Marcia, she had felt a new voice splutter to life inside of her, one that questioned the Turonia-loyal narrative she'd wound around herself since she was five. And now, Max's words provoked that voice once again. "Were you foolish, Hera," it asked, "to have given loyalty to the very country that snatched you from your own family and deprived you of love and joy all these years?" She began to feel a creeping shame that perhaps the voice was right. Could anything really redeem what she'd done? The thoughts rattled inside of her like stones in her shoe.

She hardly noticed as Marcia and Max bid her farewell. Noon was an hour away.

29

Underground

Down in the tunnel, Jason and Joe had retreated to avoid alerting the guard in the security booth. As soon as they had done so, the Royal, whoever he was, came into view, striding into the hemisphere and towards the booth. The boys shrank back even further, watching from the shadows. The security guard looked up from his screen and sprang to his feet. He hurried into the hemisphere and bowed.

"At your service, Your Highness," he said, his nose almost touching his knees.

The Royal took very little notice.

"Take the truck back to the compound," he instructed, hardly breaking his stride as he walked to the security booth door. The Royal stepped inside the booth and pressed a button. The lights in the compound went out for a second time as a rectangle of dirt descended to the ramp in the hemisphere. The security guard reversed the truck up the ramp and onto the rectangle, and the Royal pressed a second switch. The truck ascended up through the hole in the roof. Then the guard switched on the headlights and drove the truck across to its place in the car park. The boys down in the bunker didn't see this, of course, but Kia and her colleagues at XSHC did.

Jason and Joe expected the Royal to return to the tunnel he'd come from, but he did not. Instead, he walked around to the far end of the booth where it met the wall. He was in a small triangular sort of area in deep shadow from the wall of the booth but, with no downlighters near it and no camera upon it, it was hard to see what he was doing. Then, suddenly, the Royal disappeared into a darker space that opened and closed behind him like the shutting of a door. The Royal had vanished.

The boys looked at each other.

"We need to check that out," Jason said.

"A secret entrance inside a secret bunker inside a secret training facility," Joe agreed. Getting a listening device in there would be vital. "Can we get there without being seen by those cameras?" He nodded to the ceiling.

"I reckon so," Jason responded. "We need to move fast though, that guard could come back at any time."

It ended up being easy. The boys left the shower block tunnel and crossed the hemisphere to the front wall of the security booth. Then they slid along the wall and around the right corner into the area where the Royal had disappeared, keeping low as they moved underneath the camera pointing to the end tunnel.

As they turned the corner, they realised that the hemisphere had a shallow niche in the wall in even deeper shadow. But there was no door of any kind. Just a smooth concrete wall curving around until it reached the first tunnel entrance.

"Maybe there's a switch in the security booth?" Jason asked.

Joe frowned. "But the hole in this wall didn't appear until he got here."

"What about the keycard?" Jason asked.

"Good idea." Joe removed the card from his breast pocket. But try as they might, the boys could find no crack to slide it into. It was maddening. There was a way through the wall, but they had no idea how to access it.

Then they heard noises from the fourth tunnel with the camera on it. There was nowhere to run; nowhere to hide. They shrank back into the shadow-cloaked recess, covering themselves with their capes and hoping that no-one would look in their direction. They felt like the two-year-old who hides behind the curtain with their feet sticking out – obvious to anyone with half a brain. Jason grabbed the keycard and began sliding it about wildly on the smooth concrete wall behind him, desperate to find a catch or handle or something. Anything. It had to work.

It happened so suddenly that Joe almost fell over. There was an almost inaudible "click" and the whole concrete recess in the wall swung inwards to reveal another tunnel. They stumbled through it, now wondering how to close it. But they needn't have concerned themselves. It closed behind them in seconds.

Soft lighting flickered on above them, revealing a length of tunnel with a siding at the end and a tram rail hanging from the ceiling, stretching off around a right-hand bend. There was no sign of a tram.

Joe started forwards, but Jason grabbed hold of him to stop him. He pointed. On the wall just to their left was a retinal scanner.

“Does that activate the door?” Joe was puzzled.

Jason shook his head. “No, I don’t think so, and listen...” he cocked his head. There was a faint, barely perceptible humming sound, but it filled the room. Something was off.

Jason rummaged in their drybag, pushing clothes aside until his fingers clasped what he was looking for. He pulled out the can of deodorant with a triumphant smile.

Joe raised his eyebrows.

“I mean, I know we’ve been through a lot, Jas, but...”

Jason punched him.

“Just look.” Aiming the can ahead of them, he sprayed into the space, and instantly Joe understood. Between them and the tram rail a pattern of criss-crossing laser lines appeared in the spray. If Joe had broken one of those lines, he would have tripped an alarm somewhere, set off a booby trap, or worse.

Joe looked at Jason with wide eyes and shivered. “That was close.”

“Take these,” Jason said, rummaging in the drybag a second time and pulling out goggles. They pulled them over their heads and switched them on. The laser lines lit up like a Christmas tree in front of them. There were dozens of lines in all manner of directions. Getting through that lot would surely take the expertise of a professional gymnast. They stared at it for a while.

Joe crouched down and put his head on the ground. He couldn't see any lines along the bottom of the floor. The lowest any lines got seemed to be about the length of a thirty-centimetre ruler above the floor. It was a narrow gap, but not impossible for teenagers like them. He lay on his stomach right next to the door, stretching out from the left-hand wall across most of the door width. He put his hands underneath him and tried to move. It was almost impossible, and it was no easier with his hands stretched out about his head. He turned over and tried sliding on his back. He discovered that if he had his hands underneath him, it was just possible to manoeuvre himself backwards using his elbows and shoulders. He felt a strong urge to lift his knees and push with his feet to speed things up, but that brought them dangerously high off the ground. Not using his knees was safer, but a lot slower.

"Wait," Jason cried as Joe took a breath. "Your shirt and breeches are going to snag."

Joe looked and saw that Jason was right. All it would take was just an air current or sudden movement and the billowy Anasiun fabric would trip the laser. There was nothing else for it; the boys stripped down to just their vests, stuffing the rest of their clothes in the bulging drybags.

Jason went first, shuffling along inch by inch on the right of the tunnel, slowly making his way beneath the laser lines. Five minutes later, Jason had managed to move one body length.

“This is going to take forever,” Jason complained, resting for a moment.

“I know,” Joe responded. “But we haven’t got a better idea.” He was already lying on his back on the left side of the tunnel, mimicking Jason’s movements and making similar progress. Every few minutes the boys had to rest. It was painful and painstaking work. Their goggles gave them a permanent reminder of the peril above. Their backs were getting more and more raw, their shoulders ached, and their elbows hurt from pushing repeatedly into the gritty floor. But they made progress. Getting across the twelve-metre laser field took them the best part of an hour.

Finally, Jason realised he had moved past the final laser beam. He shuffled faster, nervous of lifting his head until he was confident his whole body was out. Moments later he risked a look over his left shoulder. No more laser beams were visible. He sat up in relief.

The platform stood just to their left, and the rail from the tram ran from the ceiling just in front of them and around the corner to wherever the tunnel led. After putting their clothes back on, Joe set off at a fast walk, swinging his drybag onto his back as he did so. Jason followed after him as best he could, limping, although he wasn’t sure whether he limped because his ankle still hurt or because he thought his ankle might hurt.

Joe slowed. “Where could this lead?” he wondered aloud. “I hope it’s not like the tram from Ruwark to Arelard Castle. That’s a four-hour tram ride, which would make for a three-day hike, I’d imagine.”

Joe was silent. Neither of them wanted to think about it, so they settled into a steady pace. They walked and walked and walked. Hardly anything ever changed. The rail hang shining from the ceiling. The soft lights glowed at regular intervals. The tunnel stayed the same width for mile after mile. The only change was the occasional bend to the right or the left.

After three hours, Jason stopped. They sat on the dirt floor, and Jason stretched his left leg out, wiggling his ankle. He winced as he did so. Yes, the pain was still there, and definitely worse than a couple of hours ago. They pulled their water bottles from the drybags and devoured the flat-bread wraps and Anasiun pad-snacks they had been given back at Port Diblaine.

"Still nothing from Kia," Jason remarked, leaning his head against the wall, wondering what was going on back at XSHC.

"Let's contact them anyway when we reach the end of this tunnel," Joe replied. "Our intel might be useful, even if they can't speak to us."

Jason checked his watch. Dawn was in just over two hours. Time to get going. They set off down the tunnel once more.

As they rounded a shallow bend an hour later, they found a tram standing a few metres ahead and immediately they retreated in silence. Signalling to Jason and removing his shoes, Joe left Jason with the gear and glided round the corner, hugging the wall and keeping his eyes peeled, moving in total silence just as he had been taught at the Overlord Academy. It took him nearly ten minutes to ensure the tram was empty. He returned to Jason to give the all-clear.

As they moved to the end of the tram, they found directly in front of it was a platform containing a mostly blank wall save for pair of elevator doors and a button. The boys looked at each other and had a whispered conference.

"You up for it?" Joe asked, moving to press the button.

"No!" Jason grabbed Joe's arm. "If we call the lift, someone might hear it activating and know we're here. What about that low door there?" He pointed to the corner where a narrow door stood recessed into the wall. Joe hadn't even noticed it.

"Alright," he agreed, taking the necessary steps to the right and pushing on the door. To his surprise it opened inwards easily enough, so he and Jason stepped through into a tiny lobby with nothing in it but a steep and narrow stone staircase. They ascended silently, arriving at the top of a small landing which was fully enclosed except for a strangely small door. There was a push bar on it, tempting them through. Joe put his ear to the door and listened. He could hear nothing except for his own breathing. He shrugged.

"Nothing for it," he whispered and pushed the bar.

30

Womak Castle

"It's done. Now you should have two-way communication with the boys." The sound technicians looked more relieved than pleased as they presented the news to Kia at the XSHC office. Kia wasted no time. She used her implant, putting a hand to the gold circle around her ear. It spluttered to life, glowing against her skin.

"Jason, Joe – what's happening? Where are you?"

But there was no response. Just a slight crackle from the other end. She swung her head around to the technicians again.

"What's that sound?"

The technicians frowned. It was definitely working, no doubt about that. But as to where the sound was coming from...They looked at one another. Was it even possible?

"What? What is it?" Kia demanded.

"It seems that they are in Womak Castle," the shorter man said, looking up from the screen. A wave of dread washed over Kia. Womak Castle, the impregnable fortress and the cruel Emperor's abode. The beating black heart of Turonia's evil ambition.

Xci1, who by this time had travelled the four hours back to Arelard to work alongside Kia, was the first to respond. He paled.

"Womak Castle? Are you sure?" He suppressed the alarm in his voice. "Did they get captured?"

But he was interrupted by a whisper from the implant.

"Kia," Joe's voice was faint. "Sorry we've not been able to speak. We've been…occupied."

"We hear you," Kia responded, relief making her knees weak. She had never been so glad to hear Joe's voice. She moved closer to the screen. "Is Jason okay?" She couldn't help herself.

"Yes, he's fine, up and walking," Joe whispered. "We've just made it through the Black Ops training ground. Kia, it's *underground*, that's why we couldn't see it on the satellite. Then we ended up walking for miles down a tram line, but we don't know where it's taken us…"

Kia looked at the engineers.

"Womak Castle," she said.

"What?"

"You're in Womak Castle," she said again, clearing her throat.

There was silence from the other end of the implants.

"Well, we've got out of worse scrapes." Joe's forced attempt at levity fell flat on both ends of the device. "Listen," he continued, "we've got intel for you. We think Turonia are sending another assassin like we expected."

He paused. "But they're using a codeword for it: Operation Goldensun."

Golden sun. Kia froze, her brain moving at a hundred miles an hour trying to figure out why that word was familiar. Then her mouth fell open. Golden sun. *Goldensun.* She'd heard it not three hours ago amongst the chatter of information from the listening devices. She was wrong. They hadn't been talking about the weather at all. How could she be so blind? She looked at Xci1 with wide, urgent eyes.

"Okay, we'll be in touch with an exit plan for you soon," she said to Jason and Joe, clicking her fingers at the bewildered technicians, gesturing for them to pick up their headphones. "We have to go." It pained her to leave them so soon after reconnecting, but there was no time to waste.

"Okay," Jason replied. Kia felt tears rise in her throat at Jason's voice.

"Be careful," she couldn't help but add.

At that, the line flattened.

Kia looked at the technicians.

"We need every available personnel on the headphones," she said to the room, no trace of tears. "Listen for the word 'Goldensun'."

The team got to work.

*

Finding out they were now in Womak Castle had filled Jason and Joe with trepidation. They had pushed the small door open with shaking hands, ending up in a stairwell in a very plain hallway. When the boys got through, they noticed a small "Maintenance" sign on the door. No-one would have known it was a route down to the tram below. Through the next door was a cavernous lobby.

The ceiling was right up at the roof of the building, and its centre was a huge arched field of glass through which natural light could stream during the day, although it was still almost completely dark outside. The floor was an acre of polished marble, and the walls were hung in a tasteful cream with gold detail. A beautiful curving staircase with ornate balustrades ran from the very centre of the floor in a large sweeping curve to the left, ending at a mezzanine floor twenty feet above them. There was a large marble-topped reception desk on the left wall, a huge black grand piano on an oval platform beyond it, and a full bar at the far end. Great glittering chandeliers hung from the ceiling. Elsewhere the lobby was filled with original pedestalled sculptures, the like of which the boys had never seen, huge vases of real flowers, and immaculately upholstered armchairs in small clusters beside highly polished coffee tables. Before the reception desk just to their left was a bank of three lifts, the near one labelled "Private" with a small black button and accompanied with a retinal scanner.

But most of it went utterly unnoticed at first, because running from the floor on the right-hand side was a huge, curving wall of glass. It ran up all the way through the mezzanine floor to a marble plinth high above them, and behind the glass swam multitudinous colourful fish in the largest aquarium imaginable. The floor of the tank was covered in sand, almost white in colour, with plants, rocks and shells dotted about at the front. A great reef in dark rock and pink coral rose up to cover the back wall. Fish of all shapes and sizes swam lazily across the coral, through little gaps in the rocks, hiding beneath foliage or drifting on the current. The aquarium was brightly lit, and the boys spotted seahorses, stingrays and an octopus.

"Woah," Jason exclaimed, barely remembering to whisper.

"Is that a shark?" Joe pointed.

Neither of them knew much about fish, but the form of the light grey shape which swung into view from across the front of the tank was unmistakable. Jason tore his eyes away and made himself look around the whole lobby. He stiffened.

"There's someone at the desk," he mouthed, grabbing Joe's arm.

Joe spotted the same person seated behind the counter, wearing a starched white, buttonless top with a black cape over the shoulders. He was staring at a screen and had not noticed the boys emerge through their small door at the other end of the foyer. Joe and Jason retreated slowly and silently back through the door and into the stairwell and closed the door quietly behind them.

"Okay," Joe whispered. "Now we're here, we need to plant more listening devices so Kia has a chance of figuring out more about the next attack. And let's check out the other floors and see if there's anything else useful we can find about any of Turonia's plans." With that, Joe bounded up the stairs, three at a time, leaving Jason to climb at his own pace.

Beyond the top of all those stairs, Joe found himself in front of a small door with yet another push bar. He stepped through, discovering that he was now on the roof of the building. The moon was out once more, and it was only as he looked around and saw the wide, flat stone roof, the glass arch above the lobby and the castellations at the perimeter that he realised quite how large the castle was. He walked carefully to the edge furthest from the door and peered over the battlements. Down below was a big quadrangle flanked by two "arms" of the castle which reached out to a huge lawned area beyond. The quadrangle contained borders full of flowers, the occasional pergola, seating areas, grass, trees and a stream running lazily across it that flowed from under the left-hand wing. The lawned area beyond was beautifully manicured and stretched out to an outer castle wall perhaps a hundred metres away. A gardener was arriving at a pergola in a little electric cart and began removing tools and preparing himself to get to work. Joe could not imagine what job was left to do, but then he was no gardener.

Joe turned and wandered to the opposite edge of roof. From there, he looked down and saw another two arms of the castle stretching out to the right and the left. The left-hand arm was much shorter and clearly a relatively recent build. He took his time surveying the quad, driveaway, vehicles and security until he'd seen enough. He retraced his steps to the door, before closing it behind him and making his way back down the stairs to find Jason.

When Joe disappeared up the stairs, Jason would rather have sat down and nursed his aching ankle, but he knew there was no time for self-pity. He made his way up the stairs as fast as he could and gingerly opened a door. He found himself in a small corridor with two further doors off it. The floor was in a beige-coloured unpolished stone. There was a slight humming sound from behind the first door, and it grew louder as he opened it.

Behind the door was a large room containing pipes, wires, boilers, circuit breakers and computers and so on. Clearly this room was the control centre for the whole building's heating and water and electricity, and thankfully there was no-one in it. Surveying the area, Jason had an impulsive idea. He dug around in the drybag he carried and spent a minute or two both at the gas-intake pipe and at the huge fuse board. "Good to have some options," Jason thought to himself, checking over his work. He was starting to realise that you could never have enough Plan Bs in Anasius. When he had finished, he left the room and tried the other door from the small outer corridor.

This door led to another corridor with doors off it on both sides until it disappeared around a corner at the end. He padded quietly down the corridor for a bit, seeing doors labelled "A5, A6, A7," and so on. Rooms without such labelling had pictures of showers or toilets on them, but one room had no door at all, so he tiptoed into it. He saw a worktop, oven, kettle and a relaxation area with a couple of sofas and coffee tables gathered before a flat screen. There was a side room with curtained cubicles, mirrors and a closet in which hung some dark grey uniforms with a thin gold stripe down the left seams. As soon as he saw them, Jason realised that the whole corridor contained the living quarters for employees of the castle – the uniforms were identical to the one the employee had been wearing down in the grand foyer on the ground floor. He went to the closet and removed a couple of sets of uniform. "These might come in handy," he thought as he moved back to the stairwell.

When he arrived, Joe was descending from the roof, and they exchanged information in whispers.

"Find anything?"

"Just a maintenance room," Jason shrugged. They decided to change into the uniforms Jason had borrowed before continuing with their exploration of the castle.

Five minutes later, they had descended to the middle floor via the stairs. It was very different from the floor above. First of all, the corridor was twice as wide and had much higher ceilings. Second, there were far fewer doors and none of them appeared to be bathrooms. Third, the decor was luxurious. A deep red, thick pile carpet flowed seductively across the wide corridor. The polished, light oak doors with their dark metal handles were arched and beautifully crafted. Discreet uplighters hung at intervals from the silk-lined walls, and the occasional small chandelier added to the ambient light. If the corridor above was the servants' quarters, this was very obviously for royalty.

The boys hesitated – they only had two listening devices left and wanted to use them well. Somewhere they were sure to get good intel. They spent a few minutes hunting along the corridor, but they were terrified someone would come along, or that they would open a door and come face to face with Turonian royalty, so eventually they retreated back to the stairwell and headed down to the first floor.

Jason led the way across the floor to a large set of double doors which bore the label "Conference Suite". He widened his eyes at Joe. This looked more like it. The doors were constructed of a handcrafted frame in more of the polished light oak, and filled with a lightly frosted glass, beautifully etched with a royal crest. They gave way to a darkened room, but soft-glow lighting lit the room as soon as the doors were opened. The boys found themselves in a large, high-ceilinged room with a huge, polished, wooden oval table in its centre. There were twelve plush, deep red chairs positioned evenly around the table, a large screen on the far wall and a drinks cabinet to the right. Directly ahead were large, narrow, floor-to-ceiling windows opening out onto the quad which Joe had seen from the roof.

Joe rummaged in his drybag and found the tin of listening devices. He removed two and hid one of them beneath the podium. Seeing nowhere obvious for the second one, he and Jason left the room and crossed the corridor to another door of polished oak carrying the simple epithet "Emperor". Again, they opened the door tentatively, unsure of what they might find, and again, lights turned on as they entered.

The door gave way to an office with curved windows looking out on the quadrangle below and a deciduous tree in a large pot by the right-hand window, its top leaves almost touching the high ceiling. A huge mahogany desk was sat directly in front of them. The chandelier sparkled at them from the ceiling, throwing soft rays of light onto the polished marble floor and the plush curtains that hung from the huge picture window out onto the quadrangle. Aside from a flatscreen and keyboard to the left-hand end of the desk, the desk was bare, and the room was immaculately tidy. Joe approached the desk and attached the final listening device to its underside before the boys retreated and closed the outer door carefully behind them.

31

An Explosive Escape

At XSHC, Kia's head was pounding. She was both trying to listen out for "Goldensun" and find a way for Jason and Joe to escape. Between them, the security personnel had trawled through hours and hours of satellite footage from the past week at ten-times speed, slowing down only when something interesting appeared to happen. They had seen grounds staff tending to the gardens and lawns. They had noted guards changing shifts inside and outside the castle. The security offices immediately outside the castle walls were heavily manned too, although not much happened there even when three trucks left the west wing of the castle itself at 6am every morning and progressed down the looping drive, exiting the castle via what must have been an opening in the wall.

The same trucks arrived back at the castle around 8pm every evening for deliveries. As they returned, the security buildings became a hive of activity. Crates were removed and examined, trucks were scanned, and dogs were brought out to check them out and to sniff over the trucks. It took over an hour for the three trucks to move through security and finally be given access to the castle itself. They drove back up the looping drive and parked once more by the west wing of the castle. It was the same every day. Aside from those three trucks, no-one arrived at Womak Castle, and nobody left. From XSHC's point of view, it was more like a prison than a home.

As she considered all that they knew about Womak Castle, Kia checked her watch: 5:30am. The boys may have an exit, but they didn't have long to get organised.

"The trucks," she said, her voice ringing both in Jason and Joe's implants, and across XSHC, bringing everyone to a quiet hush. "That's your exit."

The boys tuned in.

"Are they the same as the last one?" Joe asked, remembering their bumpy journey to the Black Ops training ground.

"Hard to tell from satellite, but they have exactly the same profile from above. If you can get to them in the next twenty minutes or so, they could be your exit. But if the last week is anything to go by, they'll leave on the dot of six."

*

Deep in the belly of Womak Castle, Jason and Joe realised Kia was right. To get to the trucks, they needed to find their way to the west wing. And judging by the layout upstairs and Joe's view from the roof, they were going to need to cross the huge lobby to the other side of the building. It gaped in front of them.

"Confidence," Joe whispered to Jason, smoothing down his stolen uniform. "Walk as if we belong. If we're lucky, anyone we meet will just think we work here."

"Alright," Jason nodded. "Let's do this." And with that, he opened the lobby door once more and they strode out towards the aquarium, their footsteps echoing in the silence. They had just passed the foot of the huge curving staircase before they were challenged.

"Hey." The voice came from a uniformed worker at the reception desk. She frowned at them over her glasses. "Where are you two going?"

The boys turned back towards her, and as casually as he could, Jason responded, "The kitchens."

"At this time?"

Jason opened his mouth, but he was interrupted.

"Just get moving." It was an exasperated command from someone who clearly considered themselves a superior. The boys turned away and moved swiftly towards the end of the lobby under the mezzanine floor. But before they reached the doors at the far end, they were pushed open and the boys stopped dead in their tracks. Two smartly dressed men came to attention either side of the double doors, holding them open with their feet. And just beyond, emerging from the corridor, was a tall frowning man with a red tunic and gold-edged black cloak. Jason gaped. It had to be the Emperor himself.

Jason's knees shook. It felt as if the whole world had taken a breath. All he could hear was the thudding of his own blood.

"Your Royal Highness," Joe had the presence of mind to bow.

The Emperor's eyes narrowed as he looked them up and down.

"And you are?"

"Well, errr, we're on our way to the kitchens." Jason tried to keep the shake out of his voice.

"Address me as 'Your Royal Highness' or I will have your tongue removed," the Emperor said. He had the deepest, slowest voice the boys had ever heard, and it reverberated around their chests.

"Your Royal Highness," Jason was quick to add. "Please forgive my rudeness."

"It is not in my nature to forgive," the Emperor said. He looked at them a second more, and Jason saw the moment something changed in his dark eyes. The moment he comprehended their ill-fitting uniforms, the sweat on Joe's brow and the weakness of their words. He turned to his men.

"Seize them."

The two men standing to attention leapt into motion.

"Intruders!" one of them cried, reaching for the bludgeon in his belt.

Without thinking, Jason plunged his hand into his pocket and pressed the remote switch. Up in the machine room on the top floor, two charges blew. The first explosion blasted a hole in the electrical switchboard, plunging the entire castle into darkness. The second ruptured the gas main, resulting in an explosion which rocked the building and set off all the alarms. In seconds, what had been an almost entirely silent castle erupted in a cacophony of noise.

As soon as he had pressed the switch, Jason had grabbed Joe's hand and pulled him close.

"I'll explain later. Come quickly," he managed to whisper.

Now, most people think that if the enemy is ahead and you need to get away, you should run in the opposite direction. But Jason knew that the protocol for bodyguards is to protect. So as soon as the lights blew and the alarms sounded, he knew the two uniformed guards would dash forwards to protect the Emperor. Therefore, instead of retreating back to the stone stairwell, Jason dragged Joe in a wide arc around where he assumed the Emperor stood, and over to the double doors through which the Emperor had come. A few seconds after the lights went out, their eyes grew accustomed to the darkness and they could pick out the doors. They dashed through them, pulling them shut. The Emperor's shock at the sudden darkness, explosion and blaring alarms lasted only moments. He was not Emperor for nothing. So whilst his older eyes took a little longer to adjust, he discovered their escape within seconds and hollered at his guards to give chase.

Jason and Joe raced down the corridor, stumbling because of the dark and Jason's ankle. They burst through another set of double doors, this time finding themselves in a large cafeteria. It held a number of people dressed in the same uniform as the boys. These folks had jumped up from their tables and were rushing towards the glass emergency doors at the side of the room and spilling out onto the grass outside. Joe was tempted to follow, but he had a different idea.

“This way,” he called to Jason as he ran around a serving counter and into the kitchens beyond. He grabbed a bottle of cooking oil and began pouring it about, along a counter and down to the floor. He set a charge in a drawer below the oil. Seeing his meaning, Jason ran to collect anything flammable he could find, strewing them this way and that. He noticed a deep-fat fryer and, with one hefty shove, he pushed it over on its side, sending hot fat flooding across the floor. The boys were working their way towards the back of the kitchen, but the guards had now reached the cafeteria.

They retreated towards the doors on the back wall of the kitchen. One was clearly an emergency exit to the outside, the other was a smaller door.

“Here,” Joe shouted above the noise of the alarms and the cursing of the guards, lunging towards the smaller door. Jason whirled around and dashed after Joe as fast as his throbbing ankle would allow, trying to avoid the slippery hot fat on the floor.

They were well into the west wing now, and by the early pre-dawn light they could make out the end of the looping driveway through the windows to their left. All the storerooms and offices they passed were empty – the staff had made a swift exit at the sound of the alarms. Workers were milling about outside, talking over each other, arguing about what to do. More important than all that, though,

Jason could see the three trucks still parked on the driveway. It was not yet 6am.

As the crowd shuffled about outside waiting for the alarms to stop, one of them glanced up at the top of the main castle building and cried out, pointing with an outstretched arm. Up on the top floor of the castle, a small column of black smoke streamed vertically upwards into the sky.

It was at this exact moment that Jason and Joe emerged from the corridor into the early-morning light, going completely unnoticed by the gaping crowd. In a matter of seconds, the boys threw their bags under the first truck in the line, slid underneath, located the niche above the front wheels and hid themselves from prying eyes. When the two guards emerged from the building a few moments later, all they could see were forty or fifty staff personnel, dressed exactly like Jason and Joe had been, pointing, shouting and rushing about.

The three drivers climbed into their respective trucks to make their usual departure. The guards did a quick check in the back of each truck as it left but found only empty crates and nothing more. The trucks rolled away down the looping driveway.

"We made it," Joe said in a whisper, gripping on as hard as he could.

"Not quite," Jason returned over the grumble of the engine. "We could get stopped yet."

Joe craned his neck to look at his friend.

"So you were a little busier in that maintenance room than you let on?"

"Yes," Jason grinned. "One or two charges seemed like a good idea at the time."

"You're telling me." Joe returned his grin.

*

Back at XSHC, the team had watched as all the lights went out. They had noted all the personnel streaming out of the west wing and onto the lawned area. They saw the security forces outside the castle wall burst into a frenzy of activity. From the satellite imagery, it looked like a very large man was giving orders and directing people here and there. But they also noticed, with relief, that Jason and Joe made their exit and disappeared under the truck. They saw the two security guards emerge from the west wing and hunt about for them. But more and more personnel were emerging from the castle itself, some uniformed, some dressed, but many in their night clothes.

None had any idea what was going on. The Emperor stepped out onto the castle lawn as the last of the three trucks left the castle and made its way down the outer drive to the main road below. At that moment, Joe blew the last charge in the kitchens. The boys under the truck could neither see nor hear whether it had worked, but for the personnel on the castle lawns it was a different story. One moment, they were watching the flames and blackening smoke billowing from the top floor of the main building. The next moment, the kitchens erupted into an inferno, belching thick acrid smoke across the cafeteria and out of the windows. The whole crowd of workers flowed away from the smoke like a receding tide, crying out and shouting and running for hoses. Within seconds, it was pandemonium.

32

The Sun Sets in the East

"I've got something!" The cry from a technician tore Kia's attention away from the spectacle at Womak Castle.

For the fourth time that hour, she gestured for the audio to be put on loudspeaker. Silence rippled across the room.

"...suspect that they know. Operation Goldensun, is it done?" A gravelly voice broke through the crackle from the speaker. They could hear the castle alarms still blaring in the background.

"Yes...Highness." Another voice: "...sun is setting soon...in the east. Everything is in motion."

"Say more," Kia thought, her fists clenched.

But the only reply was, "Good."

Static prevailed once again. Kia slumped back into her chair, tears of frustration stinging her eyes. They had waded through hours of meaningless conversation, and this was all they had. The Black Ops officers were incredibly tight lipped, even from within the sanctum of their own fortress. She sighed as Xci1 put an uncharacteristic hand on her shoulder. With a gentleness to his voice which Kia had not heard until now, he said, "At least Jason and Joe are out."

Kia nodded and bit her lip. She knew that if she properly thought about Jason being out of harm's way, emotion would overwhelm her. She checked her watch: 11:20am. Hera would be moved at noon, and they still had no information about where Turonia would strike. "Goldensun, setting soon, in the east." She turned the phrase over in her mind, flipping it upside down and backwards. "Strange," she thought. "The sun doesn't set in the east, it rises." She sat up straight. She twisted around and fixed her eyes on Xci1.

"The east," she breathed. "I think they're sending the assassin to the eastern wall of the city."

But, to her surprise, Xci1's expression fell.

"What is it?" she asked, uncomprehending.

"We've sent Zika to Ruwark's Needle."

33

Capture

Zika had been halfway up the scaffolding on Ruwark's Needle, checking his Scroll for updates from XSHC, when Kia's desperate voice had blasted through his implant.

"I knew it," had been his first thought. The security personnel at the Summer Palace and everyone at XSHC had been adamant that the attack would come from Ruwark's Needle – it was closer to Turonia, had a better vantage point and was easier to patrol. But a little voice inside of Zika hadn't been able to let the idea of the eastern wall go. It was because of that voice that he had already identified the most likely place an assassin would strike. So it was to that small, rundown guard tower that Zika now found himself racing. He had fifteen minutes.

*

The assassin was outside the city, hugging the eastern wall as he made his way towards the guard tower. The sun beat down and sweat began to bead on his well-muscled, dark skin. He had set off later than he'd have liked, and it had made him more tense than usual. He reached the foot of the guard tower and looked up. It was impossible to see up into the turret. He could only just tell that there *was* a turret, so he stepped out from the wall to check.

Slinging his rifle over his shoulders, he began to climb. He scaled the wall as easily as if he were climbing stairs. From any distance, the city wall looked like it rose smoothly and vertically up into the sky. But, with over three-hundred years of weathering, the Anasiun yellow stone was full of little divots and protrusions which the assassin's nimble fingers found with little effort.

He felt a thrill of satisfaction as he edged around the windows to the turret and perched on the flat roof directly above. There was likely a guard in the turret, and he did not wish to alert them of his presence, so he let the guard alone. He could deal with him afterwards if he needed to.

In total silence, he extracted his rifle, set up the tripod and lay flat, pulling a yellow-stone camouflage sheet over himself. He squinted through the sight on the rifle until he had a clear view right up to the door of the Summer Palace. He adjusted the dial, checked for windspeed and then looked at his pocket watch. Five minutes until noon.

*

Zika's lungs were beginning to burn. He had run past a bewildered Trey and the security personnel at the Needle, weaved through Ruwark's backchannels dodging crowds and electric carts, and now the guard tower was in sight. He felt a tremor of trepidation, but within seconds he knew what to do.

Gripping the silver sword tucked into his belt, he mounted the small stepladder that wound across the right side of the tower. Scaling it without a sound, he reached the base and slowly edged around the entire perimeter, ready to spring into action at any sign of the attacker. No assassin yet. Breathing easier, he entered the turret and settled next to one of the windows, binoculars to his face, eyes trained on either side of the wall below. Surely any time now...?

For anyone watching on, it would have been comical. A guard sat within the turret, hunting left and right for the appearance of a sniper, and the sniper himself lay on the roof above, just two feet above the guard's head. But no-one was watching. And the hands on the town clock inched their way beyond 11:57am.

*

Down in the Summer Palace, a resigned Hera was masked and fully made up. She looked almost identical to her previous self, except with a slightly puffier face. "It would fool anyone," Marcia thought to herself, admiring the Juntaou handiwork. Looking in a mirror, Hera thought much the same.

Fully clad in body armour beneath her Anasiun prison garb, she was now accompanied by four security personnel, equally armoured. All four were nervous, and rightly so. Though their bodies were protected, their heads were not.

But the time had come. The transfer vehicle and its escort arrived at the curb in front of the palace. And Hera, flanked by the security guards, had no other choice but to walk through the front door into the sun.

*

"Come on, come on," the assassin thought, willing the target to step into view. For someone with his skills, shooting the target should have been straightforward. He had made similar shots a hundred times before. Thousands. But this time, when the target's small form filled his sight, his finger hesitated on the trigger. And with his hesitation came a quick, sharp intake of breath.

*

Hunkered below him, Zika heard the small gasp. His head twitched to the right at the same time as realisation flooded over him. The roof. On instinct, he pressed the remote in his pocket, calling for backup.

His training came streaming back. Moving catlike to the southern opening, he stood in the window, turned around, got his feet up on the ledge and stretched down to the wall. Stepping silently out of the turret, he could hear the assassin murmuring to himself and could see him clearly, sweat dripping from his brow and what looked like a tear falling from his eye. Before Zika could do anything, though, the assassin pulled the trigger. The muffled gunshot made Zika jump despite himself. Holding his breath, he waited for the bullet to hit. Then, impossibly, he saw Hera stagger slightly but not fall. She shook her head and stepped forward.

Now muttering more audibly, the assassin reloaded his gun, preparing to take a second shot. But by now, Zika was standing a metre away, sword in hand and Scroll at the ready.

"Don't do it," he said, his voice sounding like thunder in the quietness at the top of the wall.

The assassin froze. Turning his head, their eyes met. Taking Zika by surprise, the man swung his rifle around with lightning speed, knocking the silver sword from Zika's grasp. Zika gasped and, on instinct, charged the assassin before he could reload his gun. They collided with a thud, crashing onto the stoney roof.

Zika knew within seconds that he was out of his league. He could feel the strength of the man below him and braced himself for a punch. It came first to his stomach, then his chest. He rolled to one side, winded. The man stood over him, panting, and Zika felt a wave of sickness as he saw the bloodlust flashing in the man's dark eyes.

But before the assassin could deliver a final blow, Zika swept his legs around, knocking the man back to the ground with a grunt. This was his last chance. In desperation, he lunged for the sword at the same time as the assassin lunged for the rifle. They both got to their feet, aiming at one another, breathing hard.

But Zika knew exactly what to do. He had done it before. And now, with Scroll and sword working in tandem, a shot of electricity jolted from the end of his sword and hit the barrel of the rifle, sending it sidewise. The assassin yelped, the shock from the blast rippling up his arm, but then the assassin reached for his dagger.

"Don't," Zika cried for the second time. "I can't possibly miss you from here." The assassin hesitated. "And don't try to run, this weapon will remove your arm before you can remove your dagger. I don't want to kill you."

The assassin's brow furrowed. Didn't want to kill him?

"What kind of useless warrior are you?" he said in a ragged voice, brushing his hand across his forehead and eyes.

"Useless enough to be in the wrong place," Zika responded, still primed for action. "Useless enough to sit not four feet beneath you without even realising you were there. And useless enough to let you take a shot before I could stop you. So yes, pretty useless. But you have failed in your mission, nonetheless. Maybe we're both useless."

The assassin saw the security personnel converging on their position and realised he had run out of options. The boy was right, he had failed his mission. Death was going to come one way or another. All he needed to do was run. But the boy interrupted his thoughts again.

"If you run, I'll shoot your legs. So what's it to be? Surrender, or no legs?"

He stumbled and sank back down onto the turret roof, the fight gone out of him. Zika kicked the gun away and breathed out in relief.

"You hesitated," he said once he'd tucked the assassin's daggers into his belt and handcuffed him.

The assassin looked at him. "What?"

“You had Hera in your sights, and you hesitated. Why?”

“No,” the assassin responded, a steely glare settling over his features. “I never hesitate.”

Zika let it go. “Okay,” he said. “My mistake.”

They put the assassin in a Summer Palace cell just across the hall from Hera. Hera took a sharp intake of breath as soon as he came into view. In a moment of horror, she instantly recognised the man being locked in the cell opposite. It was Kayton who had defeated her at the tournament earlier in the year. Calm, mild-mannered Kayton had been sent to kill her.

She put her hands on the bars and met his reluctant gaze. They had a good deal to talk about.

34

Turonia Exposed

Later that evening at XSHC, whilst the Xcis were tying up loose ends, Marcia, Zika, Max and Kia were bent over a small listening device in the centre of a large desk, eavesdropping into the conversation Hera was having with Kayton. It was illuminating.

Somehow, during all Kayton's hardened battle training and unparalleled commitment to his craft, and during all the rivalry at the tournament, Kayton had experienced a human connection. He had come prepared to assassinate whoever would emerge from the Summer Palace. And whilst visiting his quarters in Black Ops the night before, the Emperor had not told him the identity of the prisoner. It had never occurred to him that it might be Hera. So, when she emerged into the midday sun, her unmistakable blonde hair glowing gold in the light, he had instantly frozen. In that moment he had understood: *she* was Goldensun. Hera. His friend Hera. This was the ultimate test. Would he kill the one person he really cared about?

"You shot me," Hera said.

There was a long, long silence.

"I had to."

Hera was perhaps the only person who could understand what he meant by that. If the friends had a visual, they would have seen her reach through the bars and clasp his large hand in both of hers.

As they listened, Kayton and Hera went on to spill many secrets about the internal workings of the Order of the Dragon, but their eavesdropping was interrupted by the squeak of the large double doors. Jason and Joe peered into the room, dirty, dishevelled, limping, but smiling.

"Jason!" Kia couldn't help but abandon the notes she was scribbling, knock over her chair and envelop him in an embrace. All semblance of leader-and-strategist Kia was gone. Jason too had tears in his eyes as he returned her embrace and rested his chin on her head, breathing in the smell of her hair.

The boys related how they had escaped from the truck in the small riverside town seven miles from the castle and made their way through some woods and fields to the river itself. They had wandered the shoreline for a while before finding a small skiff in which they had paddled downriver back to the Order of the Dragon compound. It had been a fairly simple underwater swim into the inlet and back to the submarine, and from there they returned to Port Diblaine, where Jason's ankle was finally properly attended to. Kia's relief at their return was unparalleled. And however hard she tried, she could not remain angry with Jason, whatever his views might be.

There remained just one final blow against Turonia for the team to make. Just as she had done back in the days of Mary Stroud, so now Kia pieced together the news story exposing Turonia's mission to overwhelm and overtake countries in the southern continent. She included Hera's confession to the six Anasiun assassinations as well as recorded conversations from Hera and Kayton about Turonian Black Ops culpability, and one or two snippets from meetings conducted in the conference suite at Womak Castle. She managed to avoid using anything from the Emperor's personal offices, for now – it seemed sensible to keep such things back in case they should ever need them. It was a damming report. So, two days after the Womak Castle fire, her report reached the authorities in Notalia, Parlemoni, Juntaou and the other countries of the southern continent, as well as the countries bordering Turonia. Minutes later, she leaked the report to every major news outlet across the eastern world.

Within an hour, every news channel across the southern and middle continents, and all the major news channels elsewhere across the world, had one story front and centre of their evening news. There were breaking news bulletins cutting into regular programmes, special reports from political and military experts, and countless interviews with any politician willing to give them. And splashed over the front of it all were Hera and Kayton's faces. Their days of subterfuge were over. By the end of the week, the politicians who had been paid off to turn a blind eye to Turonia's plans were exposed and removed from office. Many of them were arrested for treason. Governments were reshuffled and changed. And Turonia became an international pariah.

The whole operation had been a resounding success.

35

Harbouring an Assassin

A day earlier, at the enforcement station in Ducal City, Mark and Layla had filed a missing person's report. Hera had disappeared from her bedroom in the early hours of the morning and they had not seen her since. Layla was particularly worried. She simply could not understand why Hera would leave without saying goodbye. It had all been going so well...at least, she thought it had. Had they done something wrong? Had they failed to do something? Had Hera decided to return to her home country? But why would she endanger herself like that? The more she thought about it, the more she realised how little she really knew about the curious, quiet girl they had taken in, and the questions circled in her brain like leaves in a whirlwind.

Things only got worse once the sergeant at the station discovered that Hera was an undocumented minor. He had seemed less interested in Hera and more interested in Mark and Layla, much to their frustration. The more he questioned them about how Hera had come to live in their cottage, what background checks they had taken and how much they knew about her, the more they felt like criminals. And as his questions mounted, Mark and Layla felt increasingly foolish for their openness and generosity towards Hera. The office began to seem very hot. The sergeant did promise to file a report to his senior officer, but what he didn't tell them was that his report contained almost as much information about Mark and Layla as it did about Hera. He cautioned them not to leave the city.

When Mark and Layla finally fell onto their sofa at home and turned on the evening news, they found Hera and Kayton's faces staring back at them from the screen. Layla screamed whilst Mark just stared open-mouthed. Had they not watched the footage over and over again, they would never have believed it. Hera had lied to them. They had been harbouring an assassin. Suddenly, their worry about their own fate grew exponentially. Only two hours later, two grim-faced men appeared at their door and ushered them into the government vehicle which had drawn up outside their little cottage. No-one told them where they were headed, or whom they were to meet, so both Mark and Layla sank deep into their seats, envisioning police stations, handcuffs and cell blocks.

Imagine their surprise, then, when they found themselves gliding through the gates of City Hall and ushered into a plush conference room. As they came through the door, Mark checked his step. He had noticed Xci1 rising from a chair at the far end of the conference table.

"Oh..." Mark gasped, unsure how to proceed. Should they wait to be invited? Bow? Speak?

"Your...Your Royal Highness," Layla spoke up right away, unable to keep either the awe or the terror out of her voice.

"Miss Layla and Mr Mark," Xci1 greeted them in the customary way. "Please do come and take your seats. I apologise for the secrecy – my people have become accustomed to it now as part of our personal protection in these dark times. Welcome."

Mark and Layla came across to the conference table and perched on the large chairs opposite Xci1.

"This is the Elder for Justice," Xci1 continued, pointing to the thin man on the other side of the table. "He has nearly forty years of service to our country, and is now proving himself invaluable in light of recent events."

The Elder for Justice reddened and bowed his head.

"Your Royal Highness is too kind," he protested. "Welcome to you both. May I apologise for your treatment at the enforcement station in Ducal City yesterday? Our senior officer was appointed there last month and is, perhaps, slightly overzealous in the performance of his duties." He smiled at the thought. "You are here because of your involvement with Hera."

Mark gulped. "Yes, sir. Please, we had no idea who she was. We're so sorry for making the wrong decisions. We realise we have been naive and foolish to take her in without trying to find out more of her background. My wife is a very kind woman, and she could not bear to see a young'un homeless in Ducal C..." he trailed off. Xci1 had raised his hand. He had said more in thirty seconds than he would usually say in an hour.

"My dear sir," Xci1 said with a smile. "You have not been brought here to be chastised, you have been brought here to be applauded for your generosity of spirit. I wish that all Anasiuns would take notice of those around them like you have. Of course, background checks should have been carried out" – did Xci1 really just wink? – "but you were acting in good faith. No, you are here because I'd like to propose something."

Mark and Layla let out a long breath at his words.

"Your Royal Highness, of course. We would be very happy to do anything to help."

And so unfolded a suggestion which would lead to big changes in Mark and Layla's circumstances for a number of years to come.

*

After Kia had broken the news stories about Hera and Kayton, Marcia and Max asked for a private audience with Xci1. Xci1 was happy to oblige, not least because these young people had saved not only Anasius, but his own life. His aide opened the door to the XSHC conference room and ushered them inside.

Xci1 was seated at the long mahogany table, and he invited them to sit down. He looked kinglier than ever with the thin gold band encircling his head, and despite their familiarity with him, Max and Marcia suddenly felt shy.

"After all you have done for Anasius and for me personally, in what way may I help you?" he asked.

Max and Marcia exchanged glances.

"It's about Hera, Your Highness," Max began in his soft voice.

"Ah yes," Xci1 responded, sitting back in his chair and clasping his hands behind his head. "You want me to give her a royal pardon."

Max and Marcia's eyebrows shot up.

"How did you know?" Marcia asked.

Xci1's eyes twinkled beneath his immaculate hair and ruddy features.

"Well, I have been informed that Hera was abducted from her family when she was small and taken to Turonia to train at the Order of the Dragon. She then came to the attention of the Emperor because of her remarkable achievements in the tournament, which lead her deeper into an evil programme only designed to use her. That's where I first saw her too – she made it all the way to the semi-final, a feat never before achieved by one so young. She has since spent most of the past month living with a couple from Ducal City who had noticed she was homeless. I can understand why you would appeal for me to pardon her – not to mention that she is only thirteen years old."

Marcia and Max were even more surprised. They had not known about Hera's recent living arrangements, and they had no idea that Xci1 had seen Hera before.

"Yes, Your Highness," Marcia said. "We think she could qualify for one."

"Mmmm," Xci1 took a long pause, looking between them. "But I wonder how that would sit with the families of those she murdered? She has left wives without husbands, a husband without a wife, children without a father and others without a mother. They had to endure their loved ones being snatched from them in a brutal and passionless way. Whilst Hera was, in some sense, acting under duress, she *did* kill, and there has to be a serious consequence for that. So no, I will not be extending a full pardon." He waited for his words to sink in.

Max nodded slowly. He didn't like it, but Xci1's words were undeniable.

"It's hard, I know," Xci1 continued. "But whilst there is forgiveness, there are always consequences. She will not receive a pardon. But neither will she receive a lengthy prison sentence. I will tell you more about my plans for Hera once we gather the whole of XSHC."

With that, Xci1 rose, and Max and Marcia realised the conversation was over. He walked with them as they returned to XSHC which was brimming with excited conversations about the events of the day.

As Xci1 entered the room, a hush fell as people bowed before him. He unfolded the Scroll, and began to speak.

"Friends, there are a few things I need to say. First and foremost, we must acknowledge that Anasius has been saved once more because of the bravery and commitment of friends from another world – Marcia, Kia, Jason, Joe, Zika, Trey and Max." He looked at each of them in turn as he spoke.

But it turned out that the friends would never hear what he said next, and they would never discover what was to become of Hera. Before Xci1 could get any further with his speech, that swirling golden circle appeared beside the main desk in XSHC. It grew rapidly and swallowed up all seven of them. The seven teenagers were gone.

"And I so wanted to reward them," he sighed aloud, shuffling together the documents on the desk in front of him.

36

Justice and Mercy

When the seven friends vanished from XSHC, it took Xci1 a moment to calm those who remained. Just as being extracted to Anasius involves something like a jolt of electricity, watching as someone is removed from Anasius is also a shocking experience. The little golden circle is only visible to those being extracted. For all other personnel in XSHC that day, all they saw was seven teenagers glitch and then disappear. Present one moment and absent the next. Officers at XSHC were well-trained and excelled in self-control, but the one officer who had been whispering to Trey as he disappeared could not help a little startled cry escaping from his lips.

"Calm! Calm! There is nothing to fear." Xci1 put his hands out, palms down, and continued in his regal, booming voice.

"These new friends of ours were summoned from their world to help us, and now Xcion the Sovereign has taken them back to their own country. We are thankful to them for all their work, but ultimately our thanks goes to the

Xcion Sovereign who reigns over all and who brought them to us in the first place. So please, calm."

His words were remarkably effective. As they began to relax, Xci1 gestured for them to sit. The gathered officers spread out and sat at the various desks scattered about the command room, swivelling their chairs to keep their eyes on Xci1.

Xci1 remained standing and gazed around the room. He nodded briefly to Xci2 who stood calmly and unobtrusively near the door, deferring to his older brother. Xci2 smiled faintly in response. He knew what was coming because they had discussed it not twenty minutes earlier.

"Ladies and gentlemen," Xci1 began, "I also wish to thank all of you for the impressive work you have undertaken in repelling the Turonian offensive. Chines, you have done an excellent job as second-in-command here at XSHC. I know you still hold a letter of resignation in your top pocket..."

At this, Chines, who was sitting in the corner of the room, went a deep purple.

"But I would ask that you remove it now and destroy it," Xci1 continued. "Instead, would you be willing to step up to lead XSHC from this point forward?"

Chines leapt to his feet, his mouth dropped open and his hand rose to cover it. His brow furrowed in confusion. Had Xci1 gone mad?

"But, but...Your Highness," he stuttered, shifting from one foot to the other. "I cannot. I don't have enough experience. I..."

"Chines." Xci1's voice came deep, strong and determined. "I know much of the wider world clamours for experience. But the Scroll speaks of Xcion the Sovereign not just using the capable, experienced people for His service, but the people He in His wisdom chooses. You are being chosen. You know everyone here and they know you. You think through issues carefully and keep the people in mind as you do so. We have no-one else who could do it as well as you. Therefore, as a citizen of Anasius, I am asking you as Xci1 and, I hope, as your friend, would you be willing to lead XSHC?"

Chines looked around the room and realised Xci1 was right. He wasn't perfect, but he was here. He was available. And he was being asked to serve. He spoke again, this time his emotions in check.

"Your Royal Highness," he began. "I will need all the support and help I can get. But, of course, I am willing to serve Xcion and my country as best as I can. And I know this team of officers is second to none. So, yes, I accept your kind offer."

There was a spontaneous round of applause from the assembled company, surprising Chines even further. Xci1 smiled and he felt an unexpected warmth glow inside of him.

"Excellent!" Xci1 said. Then, as the clapping died away, he began again. "Now, let's turn our attention to the young assassin, Hera."

*

Hera had reached the lowest point of her short life. Sitting slumped in the Anasiun jail, she tried to make sense of all that had happened in the last few months. Everything she had thought was right and good had become dark and wrong. But despite all the ways she had been deceived and the uncertain future ahead of her, the only thing she could think about was the blood on her hands. The triggers she had pulled, the needles she had planted...

She looked up as the gate to her cell rattled open. In stepped a tall man. The man who had first spoken to her after her capture, the Prince she had despised. But his large presence felt different now. The softness in his gaze, instead of repulsing her, felt like water on her parched soul. It was too painful for her to bear. She couldn't look at him.

"I know what I've done," she said to the ground. "I know who I've hurt." As that last word left her lips, her voice broke, and all the pain she had held in her body for eight years began to gush out of her in fierce sobs.

Xci1 paused. And then, in an act highly unusual for a Xci, he stooped down and put his strong arms around her shaking body. They stayed like that for ten minutes, murderer and Prince.

After offering his robe to quell the streams, he sat on the ground beside her and began to tell her, in a kind voice, of all that the Elder for Justice had decided. He told her that she would not be executed but rather enrolled on a rehabilitation programme where she would meet with the families of those she killed. He told her that although she would likely be exiled from Anasius, she would be reconciled with her birth family in Juntaou. And although she would have to do years of community service, she would eventually, eventually, be free.

"And now, I have some people here who would like to see you." He tipped his head towards the entrance.

Hera raised her puffy, red eyes in confusion and blinked through the tears to see Mark and Layla step around the corner of the cell, arm in arm. Their nervous expressions melted away when they saw her.

It was the final straw. As soon as she heard Mark's compassionate gasp, as soon as she felt the warmth of his arms and smelt the rosemary of Layla's perfume, Hera's heart finally thawed, and the sobs began again. She was going to be okay.

37

The Appointment

The friends found themselves back at home, each in the same place from where they had been extracted. Each of them instinctively tried to use their implants to talk to each other, but, realising the rings were no longer at their ears, they remembered they were not in Anasius any more. They grabbed their phones and began texting. An evening meet-up seemed inevitable until Kia's parents informed her that they were taking her to a dinner with one of her mum's clients. Then Trey's parents reminded him he was helping out at church that evening, Joe remembered his history project was due first thing in the morning. A reunion would have to wait. Jason was desperate to talk to Kia but, once again, he was prevented from doing so. He slept fitfully.

Kia did not sleep at all. Her mind was racing. The intensity of working in XSHC; Trey's courage and intelligence in capturing Hera; the terrifying events with Jason and Joe, first at the Order of the Dragon and then in Womak Castle, coupled with her inability to do virtually anything to help them; Marcia's brilliance in turning Hera; Zika's success in the capture of Kayton...But beyond all that, her feelings for Jason were swirling around in her brain and her heart. And, deeper still, her mind kept circling back to the coming day when she was hoping to deal with her situation and return to normal life. Every hour she was persuading herself that she had chosen the best course of action. Anything else would bring shame on her family, ruin her schooling and be disastrous for her future. She knew Jason disagreed, but continued to think it wasn't his body, so he didn't have any right to disagree.

She tossed and turned in the bed, trying to get comfortable. She checked the clock by her bed for the hundredth time. 4:24am. It was hopeless. She got out of bed and visited the bathroom. The nausea seemed to be getting worse.

By 8am, she was ready for her morning, so she thought. She tried to sound a cheery "goodbye" to her mum as she left, ostensibly for school. Thankfully her mum had not noticed the tension in Kia's voice. She walked slowly, trying to focus on the directions on her phone and putting what would happen at her destination out of her mind. "One step at a time, Kia. One step at a time," she said to herself. Unlike the ten-minute walk to school, the clinic was a good thirty-minute trek. She was soon slightly sweaty from the ups and downs of the roads she trudged along. As she approached the clinic, she saw Marcia.

"Oh no," she thought, feeling a rush of dread. "I can't deal with her disapproval and trying to persuade me and..."

But Marcia broke into her thoughts.

"Kia, I'm not here to persuade you or argue with you or get in your way. I'm your friend. And I'm here just to be with you, remember? Even if this is something you feel you must do, you are definitely *not* doing it alone."

Kia was weak with gratitude. She realised she was far less determined and certain than she had thought. She was struggling to hold everything together.

"Thanks,'" she managed to say as they walked towards the entrance foyer.

She was not sure what she had been expecting, but inside looked very similar to her usual doctors' surgery. There were comfortable chairs with a low coffee table between them, carrying old copies of housekeeping and health magazines. The reception desk just inside the door was staffed by a short blonde lady with bright-red lipstick and immaculate teeth. She displayed them with a smile as Kia and Marcia entered, and asked if they had an appointment. Kia gave her name and date of birth, and they were invited to take a seat by the window. They sat in nervous silence for three or four minutes before Kia's name was called. Marcia waited in the waiting room, texting Jason the news – she hadn't heard anything from him yet – and hoping desperately for a miracle.

The clinician's office held a hospital bed, a desk and computer, medical supplies and an ultrasound machine in one corner. The doctor invited Kia in with a smile and explained what was going to happen. She offered Kia some ibuprofen ahead of time to help with the pain. She explained that she would give Kia some medication and that they would use a small device to remove the unwanted tissue. Tissue. The word rang around Kia's head again and again. She began to feel nauseous, and tears pricked at her eyes again.

"B-b-bathroom," she managed to squeak, trying not to be sick. The doctor pointed her across the hallway, and she rushed over. It was the end of her breakfast, but the tears were falling freely now. She clutched her stomach and sobbed, distraught.

After a few minutes, Kia stood up. But she didn't go back to the office, instead she stumbled into the lobby. Marcia leapt up to meet her friend as she came through the door, holding her up and helping her outside. She had no idea what to say or what had happened. Had Kia gone through with it? Was she in pain? Kia was now sobbing uncontrollably, unable to speak.

"Kia, it's okay," Marcia said, putting her arm around her and trying to comfort her. "It's okay. We'll get through this together."

Kia could say nothing. The tears were still falling, her stomach was in knots and her legs were like jelly. She felt that her life was over. She had let everyone down and she couldn't even do the necessary deed to reverse everything back to how it was. She'd never go to university. Her future career was down the toilet. And her parents would never forgive her. She sobbed and sobbed and sobbed.

Marcia, her arm still around Kia, guided her friend to a bench on the side of the car park. As they sat there, she prayed, desperately. She worried what state Kia would sink into when she discovered that she had told Jason. She had no idea what to do next. The tears were beginning to build up in her own eyes as well.

She brushed them away and stared out across the car park. And there, running towards them with a stricken look on his face, was Jason. His eyes were full of desperation. Had Kia gone through with it? Was he too late? How was Kia? Marcia shook her head at him, but he didn't understand what it meant.

He reached the bench and sank to the ground in front of Kia.

"Kia, Kia," he began, chest heaving, terrified. "I'm here. I'm here. I'm not going anywhere. Why didn't you tell me? What happened? Please..." He had taken her hands imploring her for information, for response – anything. But still Kia could not speak. Why did Jason have to be here now, to see her like this?

"I couldn't do it," she croaked eventually, her words surprising both Marcia and Jason. Jason closed his eyes for a moment and prayed a word of thanks, breathing a sigh of utter relief. Then he collected himself and looked at Marcia. Suddenly she knew she was no longer needed. She removed her arm from Kia, slid to the end of the bench and got up as Jason took her place.

She looked back at them as she reached the end of the car park, wondering what they were going to do. The road ahead was going to be long, difficult and utterly life-altering. She knew that. And she knew the friends would rally around and do everything they could to support them. But, despite the desperate circumstances and the heartache and the complex reactions of parents and others, there would also be joy. In just a few months, there would be joy. Joy from the pain. Joy.

About the Author

Rich Castro has taught in boarding schools for twenty years. He has an MDiv from Reformed Theological Seminary. He is passionate about preaching, discipleship and youthwork, with a particular focus on finding ways to eradicate Biblical illiteracy in the church and to point young people and adults alike to the wonder of Jesus.